T0114731

OTHER BOOKS BY RUBEN GONZALES

Barrio Walk: Stepping into Wisdom

Barrio Walk is about life during the late 1950s and beyond while living 'south of the tracks' in Phoenix, Arizona. This story covers a period from 1957 to 1971. It includes attending a seminary and the struggles faced when returning to the hood. It is filled with Hope interspersed with humor, scripture, and a glimpse of the future.

The purpose of Barrio Walk is to encourage readers to examine what they believe.

Broken Walk: Searching for Wisdom

Broken Walk tells of the author's journey in life. Read along as you experience his way through darkness boosted by alcohol. See his jungle filled with branches of bad choices, regret, and crooked paths. Feel the brokenness of knowing his life is going wrong but having no clue on how to fix it. Rejoice when he tells you about the changing of his heart and the happiness associated with becoming a Child of the King.
As a young man he wanted to change the world . . . as a wise man he did much better by changing himself with help from his *born again* experience.

Walk with him and see how God gave him a second chance and placed him on the Path to Peace.

Golden Walk: Following Wisdom into Heaven

Golden Walk is divided into three parts. Part one, *Get Ready* will help the reader understand how imperative it is to receive salvation. It includes teachings on forgiveness and repentance. The second part, *Get Set* talks about what to do after receiving salvation; this includes reading the Bible, witnessing, and baptism. The third part *Let's Go* gives insight on what we can expect when we reach Heaven. The reader is offered hope and excitement about our transition into eternity. This book provides a roadmap built on Golden Steps to encourage readers and increase faith.

At some point in your life, you will make a choice for your eternity.
"Stand at the crossroads and look; . . . ask where the good way is and walk in it, and you will find rest for your souls." Jeremiah 6:16

SALVATION STATION

Tuning into Wisdom

R U B E N   G O N Z A L E S

WESTBOW
PRESS®
A DIVISION OF THOMAS NELSON
& ZONDERVAN

Copyright © 2023 Ruben Gonzales.

All rights reserved. No part of this book may be used or reproduced by any means, graphic, electronic, or mechanical, including photocopying, recording, taping or by any information storage retrieval system without the written permission of the author except in the case of brief quotations embodied in critical articles and reviews.

WestBow Press books may be ordered through booksellers or by contacting:

WestBow Press
A Division of Thomas Nelson & Zondervan
1663 Liberty Drive
Bloomington, IN 47403
www.westbowpress.com
844-714-3454

Because of the dynamic nature of the Internet, any web addresses or links contained in this book may have changed since publication and may no longer be valid. The views expressed in this work are solely those of the author and do not necessarily reflect the views of the publisher, and the publisher hereby disclaims any responsibility for them.

Any people depicted in stock imagery provided by Getty Images are models, and such images are being used for illustrative purposes only.
Certain stock imagery © Getty Images.

Book cover design by Jacqueline Reynoso
Inside radio sketch by Edna Vela

Scripture quotations are taken from the Holy Bible, New International Version®, NIV®. Copyright © 1973, 1978, 1984 by Biblica, Inc.™ Used by permission of Zondervan. All rights reserved worldwide.

·   ISBN: 978-1-6642-9498-1 (sc)
ISBN: 978-1-6642-9499-8 (e)

Library of Congress Control Number: 2023904547

Print information available on the last page.

WestBow Press rev. date: 03/24/2023

ENDORSEMENTS

Ruben Gonzales, the author of this book, has been groomed by God for such a time as this. God brought him through much in his life that each chapter was in preparation for that which God needs him to do. That is to lead misguided people to the Lord.

His hunger for a 'real' God and a 'real' experience of salvation was the seed and motivation for finding that path and then sharing it with as many people as he could up until this day. His foundation of sixty plus years dictates the building size of his ministry.

This title of this his 4th book, is so appropriate (SALVATION STATION) because this is Ruben's heart. He wants to lead people to the one, true God who provides the 'only' way to Heaven through salvation. Make sure to read his third book called GOLDEN WALK.

God has truly blessed Ruben with a knack for writing. His witty style brings out things than an average person would not be able to describe; Ruben is truly gifted.

Sharing the testimonies of people that have recently come into his life is such an awesome way to put an exclamation point on the message he wants to get across. Each one of these testimonies will no doubt increase your faith in the God that Ruben serves.

If you have not read his previous three other books, BARRIO WALK, BROKEN WALK AND GOLDEN WALK, I challenge you to get a hold of them so you can follow the thread on what he is reinforcing in his new book, SALVATION STATION.

Evangelist Joel Perales – Perales Ministries

Salvation Station, which is author Ruben Gonzales's fourth published book, is a gem of a tool for sharing Jesus and the hope found in Him. There is not one wasted word in this book. It is packed with scripture, exhortation, testimonies, and wise truth from God, with humor generously intermingled throughout.

A wonderful thing about Salvation Station is that the reader doesn't feel preached to, but rather greatly encouraged that Jesus is Lord and our hope is fully in Him.

If you, or loved ones, or friends, or coworkers, or even strangers you meet need the hope and salvation found only on Jesus Christ, this book will cover powerful points in an engagingly well written format. It also is a perfect book to gift to a doctor's office or any other office with a waiting room. People who are being squeezed by life's circumstances will be able to pick it up as they wait and read stories of hope and healing.

This is truly a book you'll not want to keep to yourself after you've read it. Share it with someone else and let them be blessed by it, as well.

Shelly Morales
Aglow International;
English Teacher, Photographer

Ruben is a dear friend and a Godly brother. His personification of our Lord through his daily walk is an amazing inspiration to me and a witness to those around him. I am so happy he is releasing his 4th book that encourages us in daily hope.

We are ever so obsessed with being entertained in every aspect of our lives. Maybe we are not that different than those who came before us but the desire seems accentuated in our lives today with all of the venues we have to choose from. I couldn't help but think about this while I read Salvation Station: Tuning into Wisdom. I couldn't put it down because I was thoroughly entertained with the anecdotes and completely blessed with the meat of the scriptures.

There are many modes of sharing faith through fun stories and Salvation Station captures the genre perfectly. Without a doubt I will give this book to those who are seeking for more spiritually and for new believers. To the seasoned believers it is refreshing and worth reading in order to refresh the soul. I have known the author for 25 years and I know he lives the love he shares in this book in serving our Savior Jesus Christ. You will be blessed by reading this book and will bless others in sharing it.

Gregory Graves
Retired Vice President, USPS

ACKNOWLEDGEMENTS

Thank you Heavenly Father for providing the insight and keeping me guided by the promise in James 1:5.

Sincerest appreciation for the Lamb of God and Holy Spirit.

For Irma, thanks for always assisting me and making my life easier.

Special words of gratefulness and blessings to the following individuals that allowed me to use their testimonies about their encounters with Our Creator to give Him Glory and increase our Faith:

Dakota Rae Perales
John Martinez
Tommy and Rita Bedolla
Esther Rendon Gonzalez
Brenda Hobson
Rick Garza
Shelly Smith Morales
LeeRoy Morales

*To my brother **Big Ern** who is waiting for his wings and a new set of eyes. He is my loyal supporter and my real life hero.*

Big Ern and me.

FOREWORD

It's all for the Glory of God alone that Salvation Station has been written. It is remarkable to see how God has touched Ruben Gonzales in the past five years. This is now his fourth published book, and like his three previous books, Salvation Station is about sharing Jesus with others. Ruben fully understands that there are many being raised like him that may never have the opportunity to hear the entire Gospel. For example, in this book you will read how as a sports fan in his late twenties, he did not know what the signs at televised NFL games displaying the words **John 3:16** meant.

This book is one of encouragement and increases faith when you read about ordinary people, like you and I, being touched by an extraordinary God. Each of the testimonies provided by courageous individuals demonstrate how all of our stories need to be shared. **Revelation 12:11** tells us clearly, "*They triumphed over him (Satan) by the blood of the Lamb and by the word of their testimony.*" Our testimonies are full of power, enough to make the darkness of the world flee. As shown throughout this book, *Darkness cannot remain where the Light of Heaven shines.* The amazing testimonies in Salvation Station will make joyful tears leak out of your eyes. All honor and glory to God for connecting these individuals to Mr. Gonzales so we can all be blessed by the miracles God provided them with.

In Salvation Station you will also read about how Ruben's life assignment changed after his encounter with a homeless man in downtown Los Angeles during a short term mission trip. God has had His Hand on Ruben and has *tuned him into Wisdom* to be able share his life experiences, both good and bad, through writing. This book is full of well-placed scriptures and recommended songs to reinforce the message about the Goodness of God in each chapter. We share a mutual love in telling others, Jesus is the Only Way to our Father. This book embraces my philosophy of finding a need and filling it.

You'll enjoy the humor coming from this Vietnam veteran that was raised in Phoenix and overcame a thirty year addiction to alcohol. He has experienced the darkness of being separated from the Truth and the Joy that filled his heart after accepting Christ at age 47.

Salvation Station: Tuning into Wisdom is a fountain of hope in a world that needs to be refreshed by the river of the water of life. *"Then the angel showed the <u>river of the water of life</u>, as clear as crystal, flowing from the throne of God and of the Lamb."* (Revelation 22: 1) Until we see the Throne and the Lamb, share this book with someone else so they may come to know Jesus. If God could do it for Ruben, He can also do it for anyone else as well. I love you!

Tommy Barnett
Global Pastor, Dream City Church, Phoenix
Co-Pastor and Founder, LA Dream Center
Author, *What If*

INTRODUCTION

The purpose of Salvation Station is to provide various examples of individuals whose lives were changed by Jesus. These individuals are courageous enough to share their scars so our Faith is increased. My prayer is you can relate to their encounters with Jesus. By the time you finish this book, I hope you will find the boldness to tell someone *about the One who changed you.* When we meet God, He will ask 'What did you do with my Son?' Only you, will be able to answer for yourself. Your parents will not be there with you, nor your spouse, pastor, friend, or children. Take time to think about how you would answer this question: *Am I worthy of entering Heaven?*

Christ's return to earth is imminent as all the prophesies which must take place before His return are completed. When the trumpet call of God is heard in the rapture, those who are 'born again' will suddenly meet the Lord in the air. You do not want to be *left behind* to face the tribulation. Make sure you accept Jesus as Lord and Savior while there is still time. The rapture will happen in the twinkling of an eye. There will be no time to pray or repent. You will not have time to run to church to make things right. You won't be able to reach your favorite pastor for advice. Besides, any pastor left behind is not worth talking to.

Salvation Station is about sharing Jesus with others. You will read about my born again experience and how my life changed after being *born again.* Remember, being born again is not a religion but a life changed by God. At some point in your life, you will have to make a choice for eternity. *"Stand at the crossroads and look; . . . ask where the good way is, and walk in it, and you will find rest for your souls."* Jeremiah 6:16

It is my prayer each reader will fully grasp the concept that we are spiritual beings living in a temporary human body rather than being a human just having a spiritual encounter. Salvation Station is about preparation for eternity. I do not want you to leave this earth <u>without</u> fire insurance.

It is with complete faith in His promise that I know I will walk before the Lord in the Land of the Living. He took me out of the darkness and reset my balance so I am able to follow Jesus into Eternal Life. Salvation Station is about sharing the Wisdom I have learned during my sometimes crooked path of life. Tune into the Wisdom in this book and get a glimpse of Heaven. May each page you turn pull back the curtain so you can fully see and understand salvation. Jesus is the only way to get back home to the Father. Immerse yourself in the Living Water of His Word so Wisdom will enter your heart and Knowledge will refresh your soul.

CHAPTER 1

THE WORD BECAME FLESH

"In the beginning was the Word, and the Word was with God and the Word was God. He was with God in the beginning. Through Him all things were made; without Him nothing was made that has been made. In Him was life, and that life was the light of all mankind. The light shines in the darkness and darkness has not overcome it." **John 1:1-5**

Jesus was with God in the beginning before anything was made that our human eyes can now see presently all around us. We cannot even fathom when the beginning began because God always was and always will be, along with Jesus. God sent Jesus to bring light and life to the darkness in humankind. This Light and Life is our Way to reconnect to our Father in Heaven.

In order to get you tuned into the right dial on Salvation Station, you must first at least consider that something created this world. The Bible says the universe was formed at God's command and what we see in our world was not made out of something that was visible. *"**Let there be light!**"* was the command God gave and instantly there was light for all of mankind! Did you know that there must first be a belief that God exists?

When we have faith that He exists, God *earnestly rewards those who seek Him*! Faith is not a subjective term like a feeling or optimistic decision.

Faith is a response directed toward an object by what is believed. Christian faith is trust in our Creator and the promises secured for us by Jesus Christ. Christian faith is a personal act that involves our mind, heart and will. This faith is directed at a personal God and not some idol or idea. Perhaps at this point, you are considering this . . . Don't touch that dial! We are *tuned* into the first chapter in the Gospel of John. It's a great place to start for a new believer or for a person who wants to read an eyewitness account of what it was like to be a friend of Jesus for three years. John called himself 'the disciple that Jesus loved' and sometimes he is referred to as 'John the beloved'.

Before I proceed too far into Salvation Station; I must warn you that as I write this, next month I will be 3 and ½ score (70 years old). My brain sometimes goes into an old man shuffle and teeters between *right now* and *back then*. Sometimes my best creativity kicks in with a nudge of Wisdom or a soft whisper from the Voice of Truth. I'm glad when it happens because *The truth is like a lion; once it is released, it can defend itself.* **My prayer is this book is a lens of truth that gives the reader a glimpse of Heaven.** Salvation Station contains short stories of individuals who have had an interaction with Jesus that changed them for eternity. It also holds many lessons on various subjects like unforgiveness, pride, wisdom, grace, mercy, self-control, and the Love of Jesus.

One of the things I have learned during my personal walk towards Heaven is darkness is overcome by light. For example, if you are in a large, dark room and you light a match, that illumination quickly overpowers the inability to see. I've learned that in the middle of the darkest attacks, I can go to **SKY-FI** (prayer) and the dilemma changes for the better. It is because *darkness cannot remain where the Light of Heaven falls.*

Let's take a closer look at the scripture above. I love how the Gospel of John, Chapter 1 verse 1 grabs our attention. *In the beginning was the Word.* What is John referring by *the beginning*? Does this mean 'the Word' a.k.a. Jesus existed before everything began? <u>YES!</u> Let me show you by going down one verse, *the word was with God.* (verse 2). Then to verse 3: *Through him all things were made; without him nothing was made that has been made.*

It gets better in verses 4 and 5 *In him was life, and that life was the* life *of all mankind. The light shines in the darkness, and the darkness cannot overcome it.* Did you notice how 'the word' became 'him' and the smooth transition from life to light to overcome darkness?

So much is said in just these five opening verses, it is so simple, yet profound.

I'm confident there's going to be some brighter days because the *Word became flesh* to shine light on the darkness. We must take in this gift into our darkest part of our mind, heart, and soul because *darkness cannot remain where the Light of Heaven falls.* Let it <u>penetrate</u> so you can have the *Life* He brought down from Heaven to earth.

To me, the apostle John, the Beloved, was a fairly simple writer and his style is straightforward. Using the term, the Word, seems somewhat casual. He could have used many other nouns to tell us in the beginning *Our savior, my friend, our teacher, the Truth,* etc. was with God; instead, John used The Word. Thinking about it made me picture Jesus as a walking word or lesson while on earth. Jesus taught John and the other disciples so many lessons that perhaps their 'insider nickname' for Jesus was 'the Word.' This is not written to lessen the importance of Jesus being the Word. It is more to show Jesus was on earth among fellow human beings. John makes it easy for us to follow his writing as the **Word Becomes Flesh**.

Note: Back in my barrio days, my friends Angel and Gordo used to call me Toasty because the color of my skin became like the color of toasted bread during the Phoenix summer. Our childhood friends somehow came up with our best nicknames; like Coop, Lightbulb, Greedy, Trick, Tramp, Winky, Frog, Boots, Pickle Legs, Hairy, Chip Belly, and Hurt to name a few.

I've also heard of a homie nicknamed 'Paragraph' because he was too short to be an essay. (for those not from the hood, ese is Spanish slang for dude, rhymes with essay) Later while attending college in San Antonio, Anthony became an ese from SA writing an essay.

John was one of Jesus' closest and loyal friends, perhaps our Lord's best friend. John was there when Jesus turned water into wine. He also witnessed Jesus' baptism, many healings, miracles like feeding five thousand and walking on water. He remained with Jesus until His last breath at the crucifixion. They were so close that Jesus made a dying request for John to look after His mother. John obliges, because that's what friends do for each other. If I could choose which of the disciples' sandals I could walk in, it would be John's. John must have worn Nike sandals because the Bible mentions in John 20:4 that he outran Peter to the empty tomb. (smile)

John, along with brother, James and Peter, had the privilege of seeing Jesus transformed before them and heard the voice of God the Father say: ***"This is my beloved Son in whom I am well pleased. Hear Him!"*** Matthew 17:5. John also saw the risen Christ on several occasions and watched Jesus ascend into Heaven from Earth. John lived a long life and was the author of the final book in the Bible called Revelation. He was a superhero and his writing has helped us understand how the Light came down from Heaven to illuminate the darkness of our world.

Last Words and Unsaid Regrets

On the serious side, I lost three childhood friends in 2022, one of them was a suicide. I feel regret that I did not get to talk to each of them one last time. Life's complications, distance and schedules seem to always get in the way, if we let them. We all have those special friends and relatives that have touched our lives in a special way. We have to stay in relationship with them to the very end. Therefore, I am committed to teach whoever I can face-to-face on how to establish a personal relationship with Jesus. Boom!

In my grieving process after losing my three friends, I imagined how hard it would be to lose Irma, any of my four sons, or my siblings. I wrote the following called *Last Words and Unsaid Regrets:*

If I only knew . . . that conversation would be our last words. I would have spoken my love a little stronger and expressed my infinite admiration for you.

If I only knew . . . I would have told you how much I loved you, instead I now live with that *unsaid regret* that makes it more difficult to go on without you.

If I only knew . . . I would have told you how life was complete with you, now my world has scars without you. My heart aches because sometimes you seem so close, but I am not able to spend time with you in a conversation or over a meal.

Life is too short to live any moment outside the Spirit of Love. None of us will make it outside of this life alive. While we have a chance, we can make sure the hearts of those we cherish do not leave this earth unloved. Love with every fragment of strength within you.

Life is unfair especially when the life of someone you treasure is yanked away unexpectedly. It could come in various forms, i.e., an accident, illness, disagreement, or dementia.

What will those *last words* be? I was blessed in 2002 because of my father's softly spoken, hoarse words to me were "You're a good son!" He said those words over the telephone about two weeks before he took his last breath.

The *last words* my father heard in this world were from me. As he was on his deathbed struggling to breathe, I leaned into him and said, "Dad, jump into Jesus arms!" He reached out after being comatose all day. He took three breaths and fell back onto my hand as I lowered him to his pillow. That was more than twenty years ago. Those *last words* still resonate in my mind as one of my greatest memories. (*More on this later in the book*) I had no *unsaid regrets* when Dad became absent from his body and instantly present with the Lord. He invited Jesus into his heart only two months before he transitioned into Heaven.

Where O Death is Your Victory?

Grief is just a passage.
Not a place we stay forever.
Grief is not a sign of weakness,
Or a lack of Faith

> *Grief is the price of Love.*
> *Death takes the body.*
> *God takes the soul.*
> *Our mind holds the memories.*
> *Our heart treasures their love*
> *Our Faith reassures us:*
> *WE WILL MEET AGAIN ~ Ruben Gee*

Be careful with your conversations by always expressing support and encouragement.

If we only knew . . . then our last words would be full of good thoughts and there would be no unsaid regrets, especially during this Christmas season.

"*Love never fails!*" **1 Corinthians 13:8**

Just A Mist

We are only on this earth for a short while we are just a mist that appears for a little while and then vanishes. In this earthly life we are like a vapor that will soon be gone. *We are spiritual beings having a human experience rather than human beings in a spiritual encounter.* Get tuned into the Faith that God sent His Son to earth so we could have eternal life.

Recently I enjoyed posting on my Carl Hayden Alumni Facebook page. Most remarks were from young graduates that could not believe it had already been 1-5 years since their graduation from high school. I amused myself by posting, I graduated in 1970, and just like that, now I am seventy. The past fifty years have gone by like a blur or a fast moving mist. There's no way to stop it or slow it down, but you can be certain of where you are going for eternity by becoming *Born Again*. You will hear about being born again throughout Salvation Station.

Here's something to think about: *Did you know that the number of years between 1970 and 2022 is the same number of years as 1970 going backwards to the year 1918?*

First time Author

When I wrote my first book in 2019 called Barrio Walk: Stepping into Wisdom, I prayed for guidance on wisdom from the Holy Spirit. My Chapter 3 began with the verses from John Chapter 1 Verses 1 and 14. *"In the beginning was the Word, and the Word was with God . . . The Word became flesh and made His dwelling among us. We have seen His glory, the glory of the one and only Son, who came from the Father, full of grace and truth."* At that point I did not know why I started the chapter three in that manner. Now I know, it's called writing while *being Spirit led*. It comes from praying prior to writing.

My secret to writing now, (my fourth Christian book) is to begin each chapter by praying to receive writing inspiration that will bring God glory through Holy Spirit led wisdom. In the book of **James, Chapter 1 verse 5 it says, *"If any of you lacks wisdom, you should ask God, who gives generously to all without finding fault, and it will be given to you."*** The verse that follows this scripture says this request for wisdom must be asked *in faith*. It is also just as important to make time to give thanks with the completion of each chapter. So, I write down the initials SDG which stand for "Soli Deo Gloria!" This means for the Glory of God alone.

Here's an interesting fact: Did you know the Latin words "Laus Deo" which translates to, "Praise be to God" is inscribed on the aluminum cap on top of the Washington Monument? You can find this at https://www.nps.gov . Additionally, the cornerstone of the monument was embedded with a box containing a portrait of George Washington, **a Bible,** a map of the city, and a copy of the United States Constitution. (https://silversightseer.com)

John 3:16

In my BC (before Christ) years I noticed that at football games shown on television there were fans that held up a sign that read John 3:16. I had no clue what this meant, nor any curiosity to research the meaning. Instead, my worldly focus was to enjoy the game and some cold ones. I was lost in the NFL world and my joy depended on if my team won. What a waste of time!

The Gospel of John contains probably the most quoted verse in the Bible in John 3:16. "***For God so loved the world that he gave his one and only Son, that whoever believes in him shall not perish but have eternal life.***" For all you guys whose attention is only on the game and brewskis, here is a simple caveman interruption in guy talk:

GOD LOVES – HE GAVE – WE BELIEVE – WE LIVE!!!

God loves us so much He gave us His Son – the Light of the World. Because of the darkness in the world (I used to be there) many have not recognized Jesus or received Him. *Salvation Station* is my best attempt to have readers believe in Him. Because "***Yet to all who did receive Him, to those who believed in His name, He gave the right to become children of God – children born not of natural descent, nor of human decision or a husband's will but born of God.***" **John 1:12-13.**

It's all about Faith as I've learned from studying the Bible for a good while now. There are parts that help quicken our understanding more clearly. This is somewhat simple but I want to fine tune your belief into the incredible gift (Jesus) God has given us. Here are three shortcuts to increase Faith.

1. It begins with John 1 verse 1. "***In the beginning was the Word, and the Word was with God and the Word was God.***"
2. Read chapter 3 in the book of John. It is about Jesus conversation with Nicodemus when Jesus tells in order to get to Heaven a man must be *born again*. You'll read about this in Chapter 4 called Nick at Night.
3. John chapter 14 gives us the story of Jesus on the night before He was to be crucified. He told His disciples He was going to leave to *prepare* a place for them. He finishes with, "I am the Way, the Truth, and the Life. No one comes to the Father except through Me."

Heaven is a prepared place for prepared people! Are you prepared? If not, keep reading. If you are prepared, *Praise God, I'll see you there!* But keep reading – you'll love the rest of the book.

I don't know how God does it but He *loves us all the same* and wants all of us to live with Him for eternity. My job as an author is to fine-tune your hearing/reading to the Truth. You can forget about using WI-FI to try to connect to God; instead get connected to Heaven with **SKY-FI** a.k.a. prayer. I give thanks to Christ Jesus, our Lord, who has given me strength and considered me trustworthy by appointing me into His Service. *Consequently, may your faith be increased as this message is written through the word about Christ.* (paraphrased from Romans 10:17)

We have all heard some version of the Christmas story and how Jesus came to earth born in a manger in the sleepy town of Bethlehem. Jesus' birth went fairly unnoticed by the world. Sure, there was a bright star, shepherds, angels, and Three Wise men bringing gifts but His Birth happened without much fanfare. Even the atheist has seen a Nativity scene and maybe believed in God after receiving a few Christmas gifts while growing up.

> **Note to the atheist**: *Only God can make a heart start beating. Only God exhales His Breath of Life into a newborn child as it takes that first breath. Only God inhales (takes back) His breath of Life when we take our last breath.* Read Psalm 14, then ask God to help you get your heart right while there's still time. Recently a friend of mine told me he did not believe in God anymore. It was difficult to tell him, "You know what the Bible says about a person that does not believe in God? "The fool says, there is no God!" We are still friends and I am trying my best to help him cope with the death of his father.

Death is difficult for us to understand as it is so final. It is final for everyone who has lived and died on this earth, except Jesus. Using scripture, I want to point out what happened when Jesus was crucified on the cross.

POWER OFF

At the time of His passing about 3 pm after Jesus had been crucified, it was like God turned off the power switch to the earth. When Jesus gave up His Spirit, darkness swept over the land as the sun stopped shining. It was pitch dark in the middle of the day. It brought on instant chaos: *"At that moment the <u>curtain</u> of the temple was torn in two from top to bottom. The earth shook, the rocks split and the tombs broke open. The bodies of many holy people who had died were raised to life."* **Matthew 27:51-52** (*Note the curtain on the temple had the thickness of a handbreadth or 4 inches and was 60 feet high and 30 feet wide*) That is a "Godsmack" display of power. Godsmack is a new word I heard today to describe something that leaves you speechless.

Can you imagine a 6-story high, 30 feet wide, 4-inch thick curtain ripping from top to bottom? The tearing of this enormous curtain was also symbolic in several ways:

1. Only the high priest could enter beyond the curtain into the Inner Room to offer gifts and sacrifices on a yearly basis, and never without blood. This was done year after year prior to the crucifixion of Jesus. It was temporary as there is no power in the blood of animals. Christ was sacrificed once, to take away the sins of many.
2. Jesus' body, like the curtain was torn so we could enter Heaven. We can now enter the Most Holy Place by the blood of Jesus. It says in **Hebrews 10:20** *"A new and living way opened for us through the curtain, that is, <u>His body.</u>"* It amazed me when I found the words, the curtain, that is His body in scripture.
3. Please understand there is no longer a curtain blocking us from reaching Heaven as in the Old Testament (prior to Jesus). There is One God and One Mediator between God and us, He is Jesus, the Son of the living God.

Also, *"**When the centurion and those with him who were guarding Jesus saw the earthquake and all that had happened, they were terrified, and exclaimed, "Surely he was the Son of God!"** Matthew 27:54*

The above scriptures are to show you the power displayed by God when Jesus died. Not only did the curtain tear, but there was also no sun, darkness over the land, an earthquake, rocks splitting, tombs opening, and holy people being raised back to life. With this Jesus fulfilled his mission on earth and later ascended into Heaven where He is waiting for us. Jesus is watching us during our earthly life and prays that one day we ask Him to be our Savior. He wants to walk with us so we can join Him in Heaven.

Shortly after Jesus remained lifeless on the cross, there came a rich man from Arimathea named Joseph who asked for Jesus' body. Pilate ordered that our Savior's body be given to him. "***Joseph took the body, wrapped it in a clean linen cloth, and placed it in his own new tomb that he had cut out of the rock. He rolled a big stone in front of the entrance to the tomb and went away.***" **Matthew 27:59-60**

JESUS WAS DEAD . . . *He was wrapped in a cloth and placed inside a tomb that was sealed with a big stone.*

But . . . Don't worry, the Power was turned back on three days later when Jesus resurrected.

POWER ON

Three days later God turned the power back on. Since no one was inside the tomb, how do we know what happened at the precise moment Jesus came back to life??? Was there any evidence of what occurred? The answer is ABSOLUTELY as shown below.

The Book of John Chapter 20 tells us that Mary Magdalene went to the tomb and found the rock rolled back and the tomb was empty. She thought someone had stolen Jesus' body so she hurried to tell the disciples. John and Peter ran to the tomb and they only found His burial clothes.

"***Then Simon Peter came along behind John and went straight into the tomb. He saw the strips of linen lying there, as well as the cloth that had been wrapped around Jesus' head. The cloth was still lying in its place, separate from the linen.***" **John 20:6-7**

*** Please note there was a cloth that was wrapped around Jesus' head that was separate from the linen.

Many years ago, I read a book called, The Shroud of Turin. It is believed to be the burial cloth (linen) of our Lord Jesus. Much study and testing has been performed on this cloth over the years to determine its authenticity. There is also the Sudarium of Oviedo that is said to be the cloth that had been wrapped around Jesus' head.

Here are some main points that I have heard or read about the **Shroud of Turin** and the **Sudarium of Oviedo**. The city of Turin is located in northwest Italy and Oviedo is in Spain. This might lead you to do more research and/or help you draw your own conclusions:

1. The 3D images on the **Shroud of Turin** cannot be recreated. Tests have been conducted that cannot produce enough megawatts of power to imprint a similar image with a blast of light. Even all the kilowatts required to turn on every light at the same time at the Dallas Cowboys stadium is not enough power to leave a comparable image.
2. The blood stains on the **Shroud** and **Sudarium** match, and so does the nose circumference and wound patterns from the crown of thorns.
3. Pollen grains from both burial clothes showed they came from Jerusalem.
4. It was customary to place coins on the eyes of the corpse for burial during the period when Jesus was entombed. The image imprinted on the **Shroud** from these coins showed they were minted during the reign of Pontius Pilate.
5. The blood type AB was found on both articles. This blood type is rare and most likely from the same person. Additional genetics research showed the blood contained only 23 chromosomes. Hmmm???

The **Shroud of Turin** and **Sudarium of Oviedo** are the burial cloths of a person who was scourged, crowned with thorns, crucified, and pierced with a lance. The only person killed in this exact manner was our Lord Jesus Christ. This gives us physical evidence is of the supernatural power exuded at the moment Jesus was brought back to life when God turned the power back on.

The references for the Shroud of Turin and the Sudarium of Oviedo can be found at: https://shroud.com and their history.

God has given us a new birth into a living hope through the resurrection of Jesus Christ from the dead! Plug into that power so you can have eternal life that cannot be destroyed!

I leave you with this final thought, how much POWER will it take when **Revelation 1:7** is fulfilled: *"Look, He is coming with the clouds,"* and *"every eye will see Him, even those who pierced Him."* This is difficult for me to comprehend . . . Every eye, even those who pierced Him. How can this take place??

Will you be ready to receive Him?

As believers, we share Jesus' incomparably great power that raised Him from the dead. (Look it up in **Ephesians 1:18-21**). It says, in part, *"That power is the same as the mighty strength God the Father exerted when He raised Christ from the dead and seated Him at His right hand in the heavenly realms."*

Are you plugged into that **Same Power**?

Jesus takes us from death to life, from darkness to light and from this temporary place on earth into our eternal Reward.

Some things will never change; Jesus Christ is the same yesterday, today and forever. *In the beginning was The Word, and the Word was with God, and the Word was God.* No one gets to the Father except through Him. God has already prepared the Way, right now He is preparing you. Again, I reinforce, *Heaven is a prepared place for prepared people.*

God has given us a new birth into everlasting life through the resurrection of Jesus. Christ fulfilled another promise when He said, *"And I, when I am lifted from this earth, will draw all people to myself."* **John 12:32** This provides a way for us to have life that cannot be destroyed!

Salvation Station lesson #1 Salvation is found in no one else, for there is no other name under heaven given to mankind by which we must be saved. (Acts 4:12)

Recommended song to *tune you into the wisdom* about the message in this chapter is **Here I Am To Worship**. You can find it on YouTube. There are versions that include the lyrics.

Here's a little something to make you look at our world a little differently.

As you know, Los Angeles is typically seen as the West Coast city. It is right next to the ocean and has all those beaches. So . . . it would make sense for it to be farther west than a desert city like Reno, right? **Wrong**: Reno is actually around 86 miles further west than Los Angeles due to the curve of California and the placement of the states.

I make this point to say, *do your research*, check it out in your Bible. Make sure that what is being preached or what I am writing is true before you believe it. And . . . Have fun looking at the map that includes both Reno and Los Angeles.

CHAPTER 2

THE DAY OF SALVATION

God says *"At the right the time of my favor I heard you, and in the __day of salvation__ I helped you. I tell you, now is the time of God's favor, now is the __day of salvation__" is now."* 2 Corinthians 6:2

How instant are ramen noodles? Let's examine the process:

Get the package.
Read the instructions.
Prepare the pot with water.
Break the noodles up inside the package by bending it back and forth until the noodles break into smaller pieces.

Open the package.
Drop the noodles into the now hot boiling water.
Mix in the chicken flavoring.
Let them simmer a few minutes and . . .
Voila!!!
Instant Ramen noodles – this is not quite in an instant, is it?

Even making instant ramen noodles takes a process, but when God is involved in the changing of our lives, it is immediate.

Whenever people are saved by God, it is instantaneous. That special moment known as regeneration or being *born again* is **free**, **full,** and **forever.** We become His children for eternity.

Being *born again* in a new birth or regeneration is an act that only God can perform in which He renews the human heart. God acts at the origin and deepest point of the human person. This means there is no preparation nor a preceding temperament in a sinner that requests a new life given by God. For example, on *the day of my salvation*, I had no clue whatsoever that I would be *born again* that day. This new birth is necessary because as descendants of Adam and Eve we inherited their sin and this sin keeps us separated from God. It is the *free* gift of God's Grace through the work of the Holy Spirit. God gives His Grace *fully* even though we don't deserve it. It awakens us from spiritual death to everlasting life.

Regeneration gives us the immeasurable privilege of being able to enter His Kingdom when our time comes or when Jesus returns to take us Home. God has done His part by giving us His Son. It is our responsibility to become born again *by faith* in Jesus. The fruit of regeneration is faith. Regeneration comes before faith; without faith it is impossible to please God. From Hebrews 11:1, Faith is the EVIDENCE of things NOT SEEN. Those who seek God must first believe that He exists. This pleases God and He rewards those who earnestly seek Him. It is all one big circle returning us to Him . . . *forever!*

Please understand *born again is not a religion, it is a life changed by God*. My change involved being able to beat the addiction to alcohol overnight after 30 years of drinking. When I first accepted Christ, I worried that I would not be able to stop drinking, but to paraphrase Jesus: *Whoever drinks of my living water,* will never thirst again! **It has been more than 23 years now.**

During my Navy boot camp in 1971, we had the option to attend a church service on base that was coordinated by a local Christian group in San Diego. At the end of the message, there was an invitation to accept Jesus Christ as Lord and Savior. Three or four recruits from my company made a sincere decision to follow Christ that evening. I saw them become instantly overwhelmed by emotion as they shed tears of joy. I wanted so much, right then, to feel and experience what they felt. I was looking for an emotion to overtake me so I could experience the sensation. When this did not happen for me, it felt like, somehow, I was not worthy. It was like being denied the opportunity to golf, because of not wearing a collared shirt. It was something I could not understand at the time and made me feel downtrodden.

Somewhere during the service, I missed the part where you must declare with your mouth Jesus is Lord and believe in your heart that God raised him from the dead. ***"If you declare with your mouth, "Jesus is Lord," and believe in your heart that God raised Him from the dead, you will be saved. For it is with your heart that you believe and are justified, and it is with your mouth that you profess your faith and are saved."*** **Romans 10: 9-10**

I was not paying full attention and missed step one: declare with your mouth. I also missed step two: believe in your heart Jesus is Lord. My hope was to go right to step three, which is being saved; it did not work that day. I just could not get over why them and not ME. They displayed salvation emotions that were very evident to me, but my acceptance of Christ did not come until almost 30 years later. As a result, my life between age 19 to 47 was spent searching for peace, but only finding loneliness and *turmoil*. During those years, I tried to fill the void with alcohol, gambling, running, playing sports and work. No Jesus/No Peace! I am ecstatic now because I know Jesus, therefore, I now know Peace. Know Jesus/Know Peace!

Make your decision to follow Christ now . . . you cannot go back and change the beginning. However, you can start where you are right now and change your ending.

Salvation is the act by which God saves us from sin, death, and hell. If this has not happened in your life, you must sincerely pray now. *Ask the Lord* to forgive your sins, *Tell God you believe* in His Son Jesus who died for you and rose from the dead. *Ask Jesus to take control* of your life. With your mouth, *profess your Faith* in Him and *call on Him to be your Lord* for the *remainder of your days.* It's a small prayer, but it's a biggest life-altering moment you'll ever make.

Then you can stop worrying about what will happen in your eternity. It comes from establishing a rock solid belief in God by praying about everything. Communicate with God daily and carry on a conversation like you are talking to your Bestest. Thank Him in advance for His answers. He knows what you need more than you do and He is full of surprises. If you do this, you will experience God's Peace, which is way beyond what our brain can understand. His Peace will keep your thoughts in check and your heart at rest. However, you must ask God in faith without any doubts. Whoever has doubting is like a falling leaf on a windy day that has no clue where it will land. Then you will know the Truth and He will set you free.

Recommended reading Romans 10: 9-10, 13 *Remember: Your salvation depends on what Jesus did for you on the cross – He loved you to death. Salvation is not based on anything you can do for Him.* There is nothing that we can do on our own accord that will gain our entrance into Heaven. No money, no giving all we have to the poor, no life without sin (there is none) – ONLY JESUS.

My Born Again Experience

Shortly before meeting Irma, I knew my life was wrong but I did not know how to fix it. Without having the benefit of scriptures like "Everyone who calls upon the name of the Lord will be saved" or "If you declare with your mouth, Jesus is Lord," and believe in your heart that God raised Him from the dead, you will be saved." *I did not have much of a chance to receive salvation because I had no clue what salvation was.* I just knew my life was messed up and did not know how to fix it. I tried by pleading and screaming *spiritually* "God help me!" at St. Patrick's Cathedral in New York City. I cried helplessly *physically* for an hour or more during an entire Mass but no one in the crowded service talked to me during one of the lowest points in my life. A priest looked down at me after the service from his perch on the pulpit but did not approach me. When I walked out, I thought to myself no one cares not even God. I'm so glad that God heard me that day. Within a month God started changing my life rapidly. Irma and I made a connection on the internet through Love @ AOL not too long after that.

I had only known Irma for a week when she invited me to attend a service at her church. In my mind I hesitated with attending as I had never been to a service outside of the Catholic Church. When all I knew was Catholicism, it was not an option to attend service at another denomination. When I first arrived at Primera Baptist Church in Fort Worth, I wondered if I would be excommunicated from the Catholic Church. Years and years of hearing '*the One True, Holy Catholic Church*' made me sit in a trance in the parking lot as I contemplated whether to go in or not. Then I thought, wait a minute, I have not attended regular church services for almost eight years. So, I took a step out of the boat (1997 Buick Riviera) like Peter, only I could not see Jesus . . . YET.

During that first visit, I sat near the back so I could observe without being noticed but somehow everyone seemed to sneak a peek at me. Irma was part of the praise team and I loved seeing how much emotion was put into the praise and worship in their songs. After that first service, I remember Irma telling me not to sit by myself in the back row because it made me look shady. (sort of like being at the corner of Shady Lane and Gonzales Street in the hood). There were no candles, nor statues of saints and the message delivered by the Pastor came directly from the Bible. I felt like a withering plant that had just received some much needed water. My soul absorbed a fragrance that smelled like rain in the desert during the August monsoons in Phoenix.

On November 13, 1999, during my third visit, I thoroughly enjoyed the teaching that morning. I thought to myself, if God can use a talking donkey to further His Kingdom, then He can use me. (This story of Balaam can be found in Numbers, Chapter 22.) The interim pastor, Daniel Sanchez, stated if anyone wanted to let Christ to be the Ruler of their life to please raise their hand. I raised my right hand but he did not see me and continued to lead us into prayer. Following his lead, I sincerely asked Jesus to come into my heart and forgive me of all my sins. So, just like that, in an *instant*, at the age of 47, I accepted Christ as my Lord and Savior. It was a crisp morning and chilly inside this large Baptist Church. As I lowered my hand, I began sweating profusely. It felt like a rushing wave of warmth, peace and love covered me from head to toe. As I breathed in Life, it felt like electricity was dancing in my veins and a 100-pound weight was taken off my shoulders. **Wow! Glory to God!!** I felt like I was twenty years younger and in spiritual reality I was because the old was gone and now I was a new creation. It felt like God scrubbed me with a mixture of grace and mercy to remove all the stains of sins. Adios to anger, guilt, shame, profanity, unworthiness, and emptiness! (How my Pride was removed is shown later in the book) My soul now was full of His Love and illuminating with the light of His Glory.

The grave had no more power over me as I had gained entrance into the Kingdom of God. If this happened to me at age 47 and my father at age 78, it's never too late *for anyone* to join us one day in Heaven (More on my father's salvation later)

My girlfriend then, and now my wife of 23 years, looked at me covered with sweat and asked, "Are you ok?"

I smiled and whispered, "Oh Yes! I'll tell you about it in a while."

After the service, I told her about my experience. She was skeptical as this was only the third service I had ever attended outside of a Catholic church. She told me later she thought I was only trying to impress her. I had earlier tried to astound her by putting in an entire twenty-dollar bill into the offering container as it passed in front of us. Since then, I have learned how to tithe so I know putting in twenty bucks was nowhere close to impressive. *As I write this, I chuckle when I think about seeing my nana Pipi putting in a five-dollar bill and pulling three dollars out from the collection basket at St. Anthony's in central Phoenix. My paradigm shifted when I considered maybe this was all she had to survive the upcoming week.*

During that time when I first met Irma, I lived in Little Rock, Arkansas which is a five-and-a-half-hour drive from Fort Worth. After my *born-again* blessing and long drive home, I went straight to bed quicker than you can say, "good night!" As I laid down, it felt like I was coming down with the flu and my throat was closing faster than a slamming gate on a windy day. Under the covers I was freezing and my *liver quivered* to the point of hurting. As I shivered, I prayed for God to remove whatever illness was invading my body. This was one of my first prayers that was not the Our Father or Hail Mary. God in His goodness answered me quickly. I felt something physically wipe my throat with a soft but firm touch. Immediately, there was that same feeling – the wave of warmth, peace and love covered me from head to toe and I began to sweat. It was beyond my comprehension to feel the healing Hand of God! The new creation (me) fell asleep and woke up refreshed without any sign of illness. I went back to work the next day with a new song in my heart and a smile on my face.

Note: Always remember, no matter what you are going through the healing Hand of God can heal you too. God loves you and can take away anything you may be suffering from with just one touch. It could be illness, loneliness, shame, guilt, addiction, or depression. When God is involved, you can expect anything to happen that moment when you ask for healing *with faith*. It is a supernatural moment when the hurt and The Healer collide.

Recommended reading Mark 1:40-42

All About Me

Prior to accepting Jesus as my Lord and Savior, I was selfish and full of pride. My eyes looked at what others had and my heart was full of envy. Even if I could have had everything I desired back then, the spirit of coveting would never been satisfied as it can never have enough. How much is enough? Does the gambler know when to walk away? How about the drug addict? Does someone full of themselves ever get enough affirmation? Also, if somehow, I would have obtained it, my pride would have bloomed with pure arrogance on full display. Thank You Lord for turning my grave filled of selfishness and pride into a garden blooming with Your love, peace, and joy.

I'm thankful that God never gave up on me – that's the kind of God He is. I had individuals like my cousins Joseph and Connie Alvarez and Carol Mendoza tell me about Jesus. At that point, I was too busy enjoying the search for fulfillment in all the wrong places. As a result, my life prior to Jesus included too much alcohol, divorce, darkness, and ME. I was deep in the world and lost with no way out. But YOU did not give up on me as I went from the *tavern to the Temple*. That Temple being my changed heart where Jesus now resides. Above all, guard your heart because everything you do flows from it. Whatever is in your heart comes out in your speech, attitude, and behavior or bad-havior.

The changing of my heart was instant and it also dried up my 30 year addiction to alcohol. I used to worry that I would not be able to stop drinking. Because of this instant change, I am eternally grateful! God always was and always will be with me forever. He did not give up on me even when I almost gave up on myself. ***"For God so loved the world that he gave his one and only Son, that whoever believes in him shall not perish but have eternal life." John 3:16*** I was *born again* by Faith in Jesus.

That's what makes true Christianity unique from the rest of the religions out there. Many religions offer some type of salvation (getting to Heaven) through works, where some think they can earn salvation by being more good, than bad. When we become born again believers in Christ, we know that salvation is not a process. It is not Christ plus anything else . . . it is Christ alone. He is not one of the ways to the Father, Jesus is the ONLY WAY!! We know this because Jesus said it implicitly in *John 14:5-6:* ***"Thomas said to him, "Lord, we don't know where you are going, so how can we know the way?" Jesus answered, "I am the way and the truth and the life. No one comes to the Father except through me."***

Thank you, Lord, for turning my shame into glory – You were the only One who could. As I get older, I realize true happiness comes with finding a calmness in your life. It is understanding and knowing who you are and Whose you are. The key to having it all is knowing you already do. The best is yet to come and worth far more than anything you may have once coveted on earth.

Just like Lazarus and Saul

In the same way that Lazarus went from being dead to alive physically, believers go from being dead to alive spiritually. We spring out of the grave and take off those burial garments. *Do you know what the first thing Lazarus said after being dead for four days?* Lazarus first breathed into his hand and shook his head in disgust as he took in the funky smell that came out of his mouth. He said, ***"Oh well, I guess a little bad breath is better than no breath."*** This is the first corny joke in this book.

Look at what happened to Saul, the self-professed Pharisee of all Pharisees. He was bloodthirsty and angry, determined to eradicate anything and everyone Christian. On the road to Damascus, Jesus appeared and knocked him off his high horse, and left him blind for three days. Saul could see only one direction which was inward. And what he saw he did not like. Paul was proud to be the best Pharisee, however in the words of my favorite author, Max Lucado, *"Pride is the reef that shipwrecks the soul."*

"Sometimes we are broken like ramen noodles, so it can increase our capacity to absorb and afterwards share His goodness." Paul, like me and many of us, had to have a close encounter with God to be broken and remolded into something useful for the Kingdom. That inward look gave Paul purpose and eradicated the ugliness of haughtiness, pride, and sense of self.

Other times we may have to hit rock bottom so we can meet the Rock (Jesus) at the bottom. I heard a testimony from a newborn believer (RIP Charlie) who told me he knew he had to change his life when he was so out of touch with life circumstances that he began eating ramen noodles dry without preparing them in hot water.

Paul, formerly known as Saul, was instantly transformed while on his way to kill Christians in Damascus. The Lord asked Ananias to go and encourage him, remove his blindness, and the Bible tells us that Paul became a Christian and immediately began preaching. There was no time between the time he regained his sight and when he began preaching. The transformation was instant and complete. You can read about Paul's transformation in the Book of Acts, Chapter 9. There will be more on Paul later in this book as he is one of my Biblical heroes.

I wholeheartedly encourage you to decide to follow Jesus TODAY. Grab onto His free gift of eternal blessings and gain an everlasting Heavenly estate. Some people are afraid of the changes they will have to make in life by accepting Christ. *Personally, I am more afraid of being separated from the Love of our Father for eternity.* With so much going on in the world today, by accepting Christ, we don't have to be afraid of the world tomorrow. God's grace is aggressive, available at no cost, and immeasurable. There is no better feeling than knowing no matter what happens, you're headed in the right direction for Eternity. **Will I see you there?**

Perhaps this is your day to make the choice that will change you instantly forever. Choose Jesus! . . . the rewards are eternal. **In 2 Corinthians 6:2 God says:** *"At the right time I heard your prayers. On the <u>day of salvation</u> I helped you. I tell you that the "right time" is now, and the "<u>day of salvation</u>" is now."*

God Knows

"Why, you do not even know what will happen tomorrow. What is your life? You are a mist that appears for a little while and then vanishes."
James 4:14

We are all just a blip in time - a mist that appears for a little while and then vanishes. Time keeps on fading into the future. Seems like I just got up today and it's already 2 pm. Saturday is here and so is football . . . 2022 is already 2/3 gone and so am I, all I have to do is live to 105. Will I? *God knows!* Lol

Two weeks ago, I celebrated another birthday. Had a wonderful time in Phoenix. Seems like a few years ago I graduated from high school in 1970 and now I am seventy. The first half century went by faster than you can say, "Is today, tomorrow?" The last two decades have seen me physically slow down a little bit, while time has accelerated. When will our days on earth end? ***God knows!***

Many of my friends, parents and other relatives have already made their transition into eternity. Will I see them again??? I sure hope so . . . ***God knows!***

When your yesterday's outnumber your tomorrows, you need to know where you will spend eternity. ***God knows!***

God knows He sent His only begotten Son into world for the Salvation of mankind. Will you accept His gift by believing in Jesus? ***God knows.***

The day of salvation is now! The moment is now! Will I see you in Heaven? ***God knows!***

If you want to find out more about how to get to Heaven, read my third Christian book called <u>**Golden Walk: Following Wisdom into Heaven**</u>. It's a good one because ***God knows*** it was written for His glory.

In prayer, confess your sins and be willing to turn from all that is evil and unhealthy. God will help you with His Strength and Grace. Acknowledge Jesus Christ as your Lord and Savior and give Him full control of your life. This is a personal relationship that YOU establish with our Lord. This takes man completely out of the salvation process and eliminates any opportunity for man to be able to steal any glory from God. ***"There is one God and one mediator between God and mankind, the Man, Christ Jesus."*** **1 Timothy 2:5** Only God can touch the deepest point in the inmost part of a person through regeneration. For it is by Grace that we get saved through faith and this is not something we have done. It is a free Gift of God so no one can boast.

There is so much ahead of us forever – a life everlasting in Paradise. Stop looking around you and being distressed by worldly trauma like nuclear war, economic collapse, election fraud, biological warfare, political and moral views, environmental concerns, and food shortages. Have no fear, God is in control and He knows exactly when and what is going to take place in our future. Jesus Christ died for us, resurrected from the dead, Always was and Always will be. In the end, God wins and so do the ones that have been *born again* into His Kingdom.

The final invitation in the Bible says. ***"The Spirit and the bride say, "Come!" Let the one who is thirsty come; and let the one who wishes take the free gift of the water of Life."* Revelation 22:17**

Jesus has prepared a place for prepared people. *When you are Born Again, your life is changed by God. As a result, you no longer feel comfort in unrighteousness. Your changed behavior makes you different and testifies to others of the goodness of God.* Make TODAY - your "day of Salvation" so we can spend eternity in Heaven. Will I see you there?

Salvation Station lesson # 2 . . . *Don't leave earth without fire insurance.*

Recommended song to *tune you into the wisdom* about the message in this chapter is: **Different** by Micah Tyler You can find it with lyrics on YouTube.

CHAPTER 3

HE SPEAKS

"Be always on the watch, and pray that you may be able to escape all that is about to happen, and that you may be able to stand before the Son of Man." Luke 21:36

The following section of Salvation Station is the most important chapter in the book as it is being addressed to each reader individually. No matter what your age is, no matter what you believe, everyone is dying and is closer every day to the appointed time to stand before the Son of Man. When your life is over, will you be able to stand before Our Savior *unafraid*? When the rapture occurs will you have the *complete assurance* that you are worthy of His Kingdom? What does the above verse mean with the phrase *that you may be able to escape all that is about to happen*? Jesus words were addressing the end of times and what is called the Great Tribulation. In this chapter, I will explain more on the rapture and Great Tribulation. As you read this, Jesus' return to earth is imminent. No one knows the day nor the hour so we must watch and pray – are you ready?

The requirement for salvation is that we accept freely the gift God sent from Heaven. We are offered life, joy, and love in abundance. He offers us His only begotten Son. Jesus could come back today; will you be ready to welcome Him?

Being unafraid and having complete assurance comes from developing a personal relationship with Our Lord. It must be a spiritual understanding that you know without a doubt He is your Savior. It has to be a connection where John 3:16 becomes personal. It tunes into the Wisdom that grasps God so loves *me* that He sent His only begotten Son to save *me*. Therefore, because *I* believe in Him, *I* will not perish but have eternal life. It comes from having the faith that we are spiritual beings having a human experience rather than human beings having a spiritual experience. The choice of becoming *Born Again* seals our eternity forever and ever. Heaven is our Home and Christ is our Savior!!!

The opening scripture was part of Jesus' answer when asked about the end of times. This is referenced in Mark 13, Matthew 24, and Luke 21. Please take time to read these chapters because He Speaks – these are words directly from our Lord. The Bible has stood the test of time because it is a heavenly book revealed to mankind for a heavenly purpose. As written by the prophet Isaiah, ***"The grass withers and the flowers fall, but the word of God endures forever."* Isaiah 40:8** Just as the need for love in the human heart has not changed over time, neither have the words of the Bible. It is God's love letter to mankind, more valuable "than thousands of coins of gold and silver," Psalm 119:72.

God wants us to know about Christ's return so we can be ready to welcome Him as believers. In Luke 21:8 Jesus warns us not to be deceived by many claiming to be Him. There will be deception and false teachers that claim to be Jesus. False teachings will try to demean Jesus as being the only Way to the Father. We can guard against this dishonesty by knowing the Word of God so well that we will not be deceived.

Luke 21:9-11 tells us not to be alarmed when we hear of wars and rumors of war. There will also be earthquakes and famine. We cannot live in the state of anxiety because these things must happen first, but the end will not come right away. We must stay free of being anxious by trusting God's promises with all of our heart. In the end, God wins and so do we.

Luke 21:12-15 warns us of being seized and persecuted on account of His name. We are reassured not to be afraid when this happens or worry about what we will say. We must speak up for Jesus in any circumstance. Even Peter denied Jesus three times prior to receiving the Holy Spirit. Peter later became bold and was jailed and flogged for preaching the Word after Pentecost. We have that same boldness living inside of us, ready to speak the words of wisdom given to us. We do not have to worry about how we will defend ourselves. *Boldness is a byproduct of the Holy Spirit!*

Luke 21:16-17 foretells of us being betrayed by even your parents, siblings, relatives, and children. Some believers will even be put to death. Everyone will hate us because of our belief in Jesus. We must make a resolution to never quit even when those closest to us fail us.

Verses 18-19 lets us know if we stand firm, we win life. This reminds me of the time I visited an elderly friend in the hospital who was within hours of her transition into Heaven. Even though, her blue veins were wearing needles and she was attached to a ventilator, her eyes were clear and full of joy. She had no fear whatsoever. When I said goodbye to her, she smiled like a child waiting in line to purchase her favorite ice cream treat from the truck in front of her house. She knew it was gonna be good as she would soon be wearing a crown and clothed with a robe of righteousness on her glorified body. *Heaven has not heard the word goodbye*!

I later chuckled when I thought about 'my church grandma' singing her favorite song called Blessed Assurance. I smile because she always got louder when she sang the words, "Jesus is mine!"

The opening scripture is a stern warning directly from Our Lord. God desires for us to know about Christ's return. I expect the days leading to the End of Times to be full of trials. I will trust in Jesus waiting for us in Heaven to relieve us of any fears about death. We have to give Him all of our emotions so we can live in His Peace now and forever.

The Rapture: God Takes His Church To Be With Him

Christ's return to earth is imminent as all the prophesies which must take place before His return are completed. When the trumpet call of God is heard in the rapture, those who are 'born again' will suddenly meet the Lord in the air. You do not want to be *left behind* to face the tribulation. Make sure you accept Jesus as Lord and Savior while there is still time.

The rapture will happen in the twinkling of an eye. There will be no time to pray or repent. You will not have time to run to church to make things right. You won't be able to reach your favorite pastor for advice. Besides, any pastor left behind is not worth talking to.

According to 1 Thessalonians 5:2 this day of the Lord will come like a thief in the night. The Bible also describes what will happen after the trumpet call of God is heard. *"After that, we who are still alive and are left will be caught up together with them (the dead in Christ) in the clouds to meet the Lord in the air. And so we will be with the Lord forever."* **1 Thessalonians 4-17**

We must watch and pray so we are able to *escape* what those left behind will face in the Tribulation.

The Tribulation: Pure Evil On Earth

The moment after the Rapture, the Spirit of God will remove all restraints that control evil from the earth. Things will be far, far worse than the corruption we face today - it will be a Godless life. There will be millions of people missing. Parents left behind will be searching for their missing children that had not reached the age of accountability. Television crews will be filming empty homes and cars without explanation of what happened to the occupants. *"Two men will be in the field; one will be taken and one will be left."* **Matthew 24:40** Perhaps the news will report it as a space invasion to explain what occurred so suddenly. There might be many "experts" ready to *debunk* the Rapture and call it something else, like 'the Vanishing.'

God will dump His stored up wrath on the earth and it will be total chaos. Death through murder and warfare will be common in the Tribulation and so will starvation and disease. Worst of all, the worst human who has ever lived leads humanity to destruction. God will systematically destroy the atmosphere, oceans and lands with earthquakes, smoke, fire, red tides, global warming, volcanoes, tsunamis, asteroids, comets, and meteors. I'm glad I won't experience any of this. I'll be 'gone-zales' quicker than I can say Thank You Jesus.

There is so much that I have read that will happen during the Tribulation that is gives me sorrow to think about how much the people left behind will suffer. Right now, God knows who is saved and who is lost. When the Tribulation comes, there will be no Let's Make A Deal, only God saying to those left behind "You Lost so Here's the Deal!!!"

God warns us about what will happen in the tribulation. He Speaks through the Apostle John describing what will happen. Read it for yourself in Revelation 6 or better yet, buy a book that is completely about the End of Times and Tribulation. Make sure it is biblically based.

I finish this part of Salvation Station by providing a written picture of what happens to kings, princes, the wealthy, the powerful and everyone else during the Tribulation. ***"Then the kings of the earth, the princes, the generals, the rich, the mighty, and everyone else, both slave and free, hid in caves and among the rocks of the mountains. They called to the mountains and the rocks, "Fall on us and hide us from the face of Him who sits on the throne and from the wrath of the Lamb! For the great day of their wrath has come, and who can withstand it?"*** **Revelation 6:15-17** Father God: I pray for your mercy for all of us.

What Do We Do Until Then?

We must faithfully remember Him by partaking in the Lord's Supper at every opportunity.

He speaks on this in **Luke 22:19-20** *"And He took bread, gave thanks, and broke it, and gave it to them, saying, "This is my body given for you; do this in remembrance of me." In the same way, after the supper he took the cup, saying, "This cup is the new covenant in my blood, which is poured out for you."*

Many years ago in Phoenix AZ, I attended catechism in a small church named Our Lady of Fatima. I was an extremely active young boy who loved the time at recess. It was difficult for me to settle down after recess when they brought us inside the church to cool down. The nuns would instruct us to be quiet because Jesus was there on the altar inside the tabernacle. I had no clue what the word tabernacle meant. I had not yet made my first holy communion and had not been taught that the communion hosts had been transformed into the Body of Christ. I used to stare for lengthy periods at the gold box under the large cross that held the statute of Jesus crucified. It was impossible for me to comprehend how Jesus could fit into that little gold box.

Many years later, I was a young man who assisted the priest with the serving of communion. This was an honor for me to have this responsibility. I smile as I think about the young children who would come up with their parents for a blessing. It was special for me to touch their foreheads with the shape of a cross and say, "May you always know that Jesus loves you!"

There was an unfortunate incident that took place one time when I was dispensing communion. A woman with a muscular disorder came up and tipped the chalice that I was serving from. Several communion hosts fell to the floor. The entire church seemed to hold its collective breath. The priest stopped the service and picked up the hosts, I was paralyzed with a feeling of failure. It was my worst nightmare without my eyes being closed as everyone watched. The priest also covered the areas with large cloths where the hosts had landed. He did this to mark the areas so no particles of the hosts remained after his thorough cleansing that would take place later.

After leaving church, I went home and cried in the privacy of my solitude. I considered inflicting self-punishment by hitting myself with a belt for letting this occur. After a couple of days, I called the priest and told him I no longer wanted to serve communion. He reassured me it was not my fault and convinced me to continue to be his assistant.

It comforted me to read His words were ***do this in remembrance of me***. Sharing his supper makes Christ followers remember the suffering Jesus endured for our salvation.

Read The Bible Daily

Just this past week I was encouraged with another example of how real the words in the Bible are. It was reported on January 3, 2023 that the Pool of Siloam will be open to the public in Jerusalem after 2,000 Years. You can read about this at https://greekreporter.com/2023/01/pool-siloam. The Pool of Siloam, where Jesus is said to have healed a blind man, will soon be open to the public for the first time after approximately two thousand years.

The pool is cherished by both Christians and Jews and is the location of the Biblical miracle found in the book of John Chapter 9. In this story Jesus heals a man who had been blind from birth. Jesus spits on the ground, makes mud and puts this mud on the man's eyes. *"Jesus told him, "Go wash in the Pool of Siloam." So, the man went and washed, and came home seeing."* **John 9:7**

The pool, located in the southern part of the City of David archaeological site in Jerusalem, is currently being excavated by archaeologists and will either be opened to the public piece by piece or once the entire site is unearthed. Plans to open up the Pool of Siloam were announced just before the new year by the Israel Antiquities Authority, the Israel National Parks Authority and the City of David Foundation.

The site was built around 2,700 years ago as part of Jerusalem's water system in the eighth century B.C. It served as a reservoir for the Gihon Spring from which water was diverted and stored in underground tunnels.

Traditionally, the Christian site of the Pool of Siloam was the pool and church that were built by the Byzantine empress Eudocia (c. 400–460 A.D.) to commemorate the miracle recounted in the New Testament. However, the exact location of the original pool as it existed during the time of Jesus remained a mystery until June 2004.

Until 2004, the pool and church built by Byzantine empress Eudocia to commemorate the site was thought by some Bible believers to have likely been the Pool of Siloam. In fact, many "experts" doubted the existence of the Pool of Siloam, period. Many of these "experts" also doubted the authenticity of the entire gospel of John, thinking that it was written long after the Apostle John had died, and was largely a book of legend and fiction.

So, I present the Pool of Siloam as current news and evidence to show that the Bible is real and alive because *He speaks.*

Guard Your Heart

"Above all else, guard your heart, for everything you do flows from it." **Proverbs 4:23** Whatever is in your heart comes out in your speech, attitude, and behavior or bad-havior.

It is said that when we open and read from our Bible, *He speaks.* King Solomon followed the verse above with instructions to keep our mouths free of perversity and to keep corrupt talk from our lips in **Proverbs 4:24**. When he refers to guarding the heart, he really means the inner thoughts, feelings, desires, will, and decisions. This is how a person is hardwired, it is their innermost core. There are other verses in the Bible that point out our thoughts are connected to our heart and often dictate who we become. Therefore, God judges the heart (our inward appearance) rather than our outward appearance. It is critical to get the Word into your heart so when temptation comes, you know what to do. In **Psalms 119:11**, it says, *"I have hidden Your word in my heart that I might not sin against You."*

Just as there are so many things that can affect the physical heart, there are many disorders of the spiritual heart that can impair growth and development of a believer. Atherosclerosis is a hardening of the arteries because of accumulated cholesterol and scars that occur in the artery walls. Hardening of the spiritual heart can also occur. Hardening of the heart occurs when we are presented with God's truth, and we refuse to acknowledge or accept it. Personally, I did not want to listen when other believers told me about Jesus. This caused me to make bad choices as I went through life. I am thankful God uses all things for the good for those who love Him.

The Pharaoh's Hard Heart

Egypt was wracked with one calamity after another when the pharaoh refused to release the Israelites from their bondage. He hardened his heart against the truth that God intended to deliver His people from Egypt (You can read about this in **Exodus 7:22; 8:32; 9:34**). In **Psalm 95:7–8**, King David begged his people not to harden their hearts in rebellion against God as they did in the wilderness. The pharaoh's denial of God caused his heart to harden. This hardening works like cholesterol and blocks spiritual blood flow. It keeps a believer from having a free flow of God's peace and blessings that come from obedience. Guarding against a rebellious spirit and cultivating a spirit of submissive obedience to God's Word, therefore, is the *first* step in guarding the heart.

Many years ago, I remember my father being diagnosed with a heart murmur. At the time I did not understand what that meant. Heart murmurs are abnormal flow patterns due to faulty heart valves or like my father would say, a 'leaky valve'. Heart valves act as strong, watertight doors (Navy term) to prevent the backward flow of blood into the heart. Spiritual heart murmurs occur when believers engage in complaining, gossip, rumors, disputes, and being malcontent. Believers are instructed many times to avoid grumbling, ingratitude, murmuring, and complaining (**Exodus 16:3; John 6:43; Philippians 2:14**). If we engage in these activities, believers shift their focus away from the plans, purposes, and prior blessings of God to the things of the world. God sees this as a lack of faith, and without faith, it is impossible to please God (**Hebrews 11:6**). Instead, Christians are instructed to strive for contentment in all things, trusting in God to provide what is needed in His good time (**Hebrews 13:5**). Guarding against a complaining spirit and cultivating a spirit of gratitude and trust is the *second* step toward guarding the heart.

During a difficult time in my life, I went to the doctor's and was diagnosed with an irregular heartbeat and possible sleep apnea. The solution was to put me on more medication that caused moodiness, confusion, dizziness, and unexpected drops in my blood glucose levels. Now I was fighting against reactions to new medications and expecting miraculous results. My work schedule did not allow time for eating healthy or exercising. Everything was fast and every task had a deadline when I worked at USPS Headquarters in Washington DC. There were times I would have to figure out which failed work assignment would cause the most damage. It was like having to choose to die by drinking poison or jumping into a pot of boiling water. More medication was not the answer and it nearly killed me. My long term healing came from a lifestyle change.

In the spiritual sense, I equate this to someone who is seeking God but they end up in the wrong religion or religious practice. Satan does not want man to obey God but to become their own god . . . determining for himself reality, meaning of life, and ethics. This might include the practice of sorcery or New Age mysticism. That person may get involved somewhere where the leader is glorified rather than God. Maybe the leader is preaching what itchy ears want to hear where everything is permissible. Perhaps the person who is seeking gets so engrossed in church activities that there is no time for Bible based learning. Get into the Word of God daily – it is a lifestyle change. Remember, being born again is not a religion but a life changed by God.

Accept Jesus as Lord and sincerely ask Him to come reside in your heart. When He makes residence in the temple of your heart, there is no room for anger, pride, or temptation. Then, instead of out of the abundance of your heart the mouth speaks; it then becomes out of the abundance of your heart **He speaks**. There is nothing more disappointing than hearing a believer engage in vulgarity or profanity when they are around non-believers. It hurts their testimony and makes the non-believer think ungodly language is acceptable. Remember, Jesus ate with sinners but He did not *sin* with sinners. He did not act like them or talk like them. *A professed follower of Christ tarnishes or polishes their testimony by the words that come out of their mouths.* As Christians we need to be a good example rather than to seek the approval of the world by blending in with them. We must not just go along with ungodliness just to get along with unbelievers.

Lastly, the apostle Paul instructs us, ***"Finally, brothers and sisters, whatever is true, whatever is right, whatever is pure, whatever is lovely, whatever is admirable – if anything is excellent or praiseworthy – think about such things." Philippians 4:8*** Dwelling on these things helps build a guard fence around our hearts. That way when temptation knocks on the door of your heart, Jesus answers the door for you. Guarding against a profanity laced spirit and cultivating a spirit that speaks what is admirable is the *third step* toward guarding the heart.

Be A Witness

Jesus made his last promise to his disciples just before ascending into Heaven. His departure from Earth can be found in the book of Acts in Chapter 1. He commanded them not to depart from Jerusalem, but to wait for the Promise (Holy Spirit) of the Father. *And Jesus said to them, "It is not for you to know times or seasons which the Father has put in His own authority. But you shall receive power when the Holy Spirit has come upon you; and you shall be witnesses to Me in Jerusalem, and in all Judea and Samaria, and to the end of the earth." Acts 1:7-8*

After He had spoken this, Jesus was taken up and a cloud surrounded Him while the disciples watched with their very eyes. The story mentions two men in white apparel appeared and stood by the disciples as they gazed into Heaven. These two men dressed in white said, *"Men of Galilee, why do you stand here looking into the sky? This same Jesus, who has been taken from you into Heaven, will come back in the same way you have seen Him go into Heaven." Acts 1:11*

The disciples returned to Jerusalem and soon received a visit from the Holy Spirit at Pentecost. They were filled with boldness to preach the Gospel. As believers, we have the Holy Spirit inside of us. We must witness urgently as we only have a set amount of time to work in the sharing of the gospel. Be bold, we have that same power that rose Jesus from the grave. We must speak with excitement and conviction so people may hear and believe the Good News about Jesus. Remember, *boldness is a byproduct of the Holy Spirt*. God does not want one person to miss going Home.

There have been times when I've talk to others about Jesus, and we have different opinions. This is when I need to stay in the spirit of Love and tell what believing in Christ has done for my life. I've learned to recognize when people don't want to hear about it, so I save the good news for another day. Often times I may tell them a story or drop a seed just to give them something to think about. It is a travesty when people just follow beliefs that have no Biblical foundation. It is also an injustice when those who preach the Word do it solely for monetary gain. It is critical for all of us to stay grounded on the Word of God. When you are not sure on what someone has taught, open your Bible, the Truth is there . . . He Speaks. Look in the Bible to see, What did Jesus say – WDJS. (I use WDJS to imitate the bracelets WWJD meaning What Would Jesus Do) The more you read the scriptures and let it penetrate into your heart and soul, the better you become equipped to share His Love with others.

"The Mighty One, God, the Lord, SPEAKS and summons the earth from the rising of the sun to where it sets. **Psalms 50:1** *He Speaks* and so must we. Are you listening? Are you telling others of Jesus? Today might be the day He returns.

Salvation Station lesson #3 Establish a personal relationship with Jesus and then share the Good News with everyone at every opportunity.

Recommended song to *tune you into the wisdom* about the message in this chapter is: **Word of God Speak** by Mercy Me You can find it on YouTube. There are versions that include the lyrics.

CHAPTER 4

NICK AT NIGHT

"He (Nicodemus) came to Jesus <u>at night</u> and said, Rabbi, we know that you are a teacher who has come from God. For no one could perform the signs you are doing if God were not with him." John 3:2

One of my favorite Bible characters is Nicodemus, who I have nicknamed Nick at Night. The Bible introduces us to Nicodemus in the Gospel of John chapter 3. John is the only gospel author to write of Nicodemus, as Matthew, Mark and Luke do not mention Nicodemus. *Maybe because Jesus was so close to John, Jesus only told John about His conversation with Nicodemus.*

Nicodemus was a member of the Pharisees who taught the Law of Moses (also called Old Testament Law, Mosaic Law or just The Law). These teachings regulated almost every aspect of Jewish life and came with a high level of legalism. Nicodemus was also part of the ruling body of the Jews as he belonged to the Sanhedrin. Nicodemus was not just a Pharisee, but a ruler of the Pharisees, which was one of the most powerful positions to hold in Jewish society. In other words, he was at the upper echelon in his job level of 'Phariseehood.'

He came to Jesus *at night* perhaps not wanting anyone to see him meeting with Jesus. *Is it possible he was sent by the Pharisees to find out more about Jesus?* Note: This took place early in Jesus' ministry so Nicodemus had already heard about some of the miracles Jesus had performed like the changing of water into wine. Maybe Nicodemus himself wanted to know if Jesus was *really* the Messiah. Only God knows why Nicodemus went to visit Jesus at night.

Perhaps there are some of you readers that are like Nicodemus. Perhaps you approach Jesus with fear, pride, or uncertainty about what your future will be like after an encounter with the Light of the World. Maybe you don't want *your homies* to see you seeking Jesus. Who are you trying to please - man, or God? Don't worry, Jesus will not force you to meet with Him. He already knows you better than anyone else does. He loves you more than anyone ever will. Let His Light shine into every dark area of your life so he can reveal, heal, and show you His perfect truth. Let Him lead you, ***"Then you will know the truth and the truth will set you free."*** **John 8:32** *Darkness cannot remain where the Light of Heaven falls.*

Many battles have been won under the cover of *night*fall. I watch reruns of The Rifleman regularly and it always seems like the bad guys get overtaken during the dark of night. There have also been many clandestine meetings at night so those participating can go undetected. In doing so, Nick *at night* and Jesus have a close encounter where the physical and spiritual realms collide.

The Apostle John writes about their meeting, ***"Now there was a man of the Pharisees, named Nicodemus, a ruler of the Jews; this man came to Jesus by night and said to Him, 'Rabbi, we know that You have come from God as a teacher; for no one can do these signs that You do unless God is with him.' (John 3:1-2)***

Jesus replies to Nicodemus that no one can see the Kingdom of God unless they are *born again*. Nicodemus is confused and asks, "How can a man be born again when they are old?" "How can a man re-enter his mother's womb a second time to be born?" Nicodemus was asking questions from the physical sense as Jesus was giving answers from the spiritual realm. Jesus also said the Spirit gives birth to the spirit and so it is with everyone born of the spirit. Nicodemus asked, "How can this be?" as he was still in the dark. In this conversation, John writes the most referenced scripture in the Bible. "***For God so loved the world that He gave us His only begotten Son. Whoever believes in Him shall not perish but have everlasting life***." **John 3:16**

Special note - Open your Bible and read John 3:16. Are the letters printed in the color red? In many Bibles the words in the color red are to indicate these words were spoken by Jesus. Our Savior is known as The Truth – Believe in Him and His words in red.

I'm sure Nicodemus head was spinning after his meeting with Jesus. He knew Jesus was from God based on the miracles our Lord was performing but he did not understand the concept of being *born again*. Personally, I received Jesus and was saved but did not fully understand salvation until several months later.

It happened while I was out with a pastor in McAllen, Texas on a Saturday morning while we were going house-to-house telling people of the good news. My job as a new Christian was to pray as the pastor presented the plan of salvation. When Pastor said the words, *"Look there He is the Lamb of God who takes away the sin of the world!"* Those words crashed into my spirit like being smacked with a really thick Bible. My jaw dropped and my head automatically snapped to the left as I turned to stare at Pastor; I finally understood! As simple as the lesson is, I finally knew that Jesus *paid all of our sin in full* by dying on the cross.

No longer was there a need for blood sacrifices like those in the Old Testament (before Jesus). Jesus was the ultimate and only sacrifice needed for the atonement of our sins. I literally ran home after my time with Pastor to tell Irma what I had learned. I had to tell her about my learning that Jesus through His death on the Cross paid for our sins once and for all. I no longer had to confess to a priest and do penance before my sins were forgiven. No more worries about the teaching of missing a weekly church service on Sunday was a 'mortal' sin. JESUS PAID IT ALL IN FULL – The Truth broke the chains, plainly and simply!

Flashback: Back in the barrio, our gang of traviesos (mischievous boys) would meet after confession to compare "who got the most penance" from the priest. We would exaggerate and say things like "I have to pray five rosaries and then leave the church on my knees all the way to Alkire Park." One of the best falsehoods finished with: "and I have to cut the grass in front of the church before Mass tomorrow morning."

We even sinned after going to confession by lying about the penance the priest gave us for our sins that week. We tried to impress each other as if having the most restitution to pay somehow raised our status as a travieso.

Irma had been a Christ follower all her life and, like me, she also experienced the complete joy of the Lord that day. Even though she had accepted Christ many years before, her church teachings had to do more with emotions and feelings instead of just Christ alone. She finally understood and the Truth has set us free.

We don't know if Nicodemus had any more conversations with Jesus. Did Nicodemus resign from the Pharisees? Maybe he was impeached and banned from the Sanhedrin. Nicodemus was there after the crucifixion to take Jesus' dead body off the cross and helped prepare it for burial. They used *"a mixture of myrrh and aloes, about a hundred pounds weight. So, they took the body of Jesus and bound it in linen wrappings with the spices, as is the burial custom of the Jews."* **John 19:39-40**. Joseph of Arimathea was with Nicodemus.

A member of the Pharisees would not have cared about the dead body of an enemy. Nicodemus as evidenced by his actions became a follower of Christ. He did it although there was no cover of *night*. He was unashamed and faith was on full display in daylight when he helped take Jesus off the cross and bury him. This took courage as he blatantly disregarded what the Pharisees thought of him. Nicodemus showed his absolute Faith on display that Jesus was the Son of God. Nicodemus showed his Truth colors in broad daylight: He was no longer **Nick at Night**. He demonstrated that *Darkness cannot remain where the Light of Heaven falls.*

Perhaps like Nicodemus, you want to believe in Jesus but you have the pressure of religions that teach of other ways to go to Heaven. Maybe the church you attend is the only one you have ever known because that's where your parents went. Perhaps you have been taught to follow other principles that do not include Jesus as the Messiah. ***Always remember, Born Again is not a religion, it is a life changed by God.***

The purpose of Salvation Station is to provide various examples of individuals whose lives were changed by Jesus. These individuals are courageous enough to share their scars so our Faith is increased. My prayer is you can relate to their encounters with Jesus. By the time you finish this book, I hope you will find the boldness to tell someone *about the One who changed you.* When we meet God, He will ask 'what did you do with my Son?' Only you, will be able to answer for yourself. Your parents will not be there with you, nor your spouse, pastor, friend, or children. Take time to think about how you would answer this question: *Am I worthy of entering Heaven?*

It Begins with Unshakable Faith

"If I could only touch that garment!" The unnamed woman with an issue of blood felt cut off from God and by man. She had spent all she had on medical experts. The doctors offered her no hope, but she knew that Jesus was in town. Due to His popularity for healing the sick, there was a large crowd around him. She believed wholeheartedly that if she could just touch the hem of His garment, she would be healed. When she reached out to Jesus in faith, she was instantly rewarded with a supernatural release of power from the Son of God into her life. What an awesome miracle she received as Jesus said to her, ***"Daughter, your faith has healed you. Go in peace and be freed from your suffering."*** (**Mark. 5:34**)

If you are going to join me in following Jesus into heaven, it begins with *unshakable faith.* If you need comfort from your suffering, reach out and touch the hem of His garment. This isn't just for physical healing, it includes any challenge you may be facing, for instance, finances, addiction, or a broken relationship. It begins by establishing a personal relationship with Him. When you have taken your last breath on Earth, it is just you and Him. Confession to man will not be your ticket to get inside the Gates of Heaven. No act of generosity, compassion, or service will get you in. It is belief and having *unshakable faith* that God sent His Son Jesus from Heaven.

You must believe that Jesus paid it all for us by giving up His life for us on Calvary. You must come to know **He is the only way to the Father. Jesus is the only One God sent down from Heaven to save us. He proved it by resurrecting from the dead and ascending into Heaven.** He is seated at the right hand of the Father waiting for us with arms reaching for us. Jesus is in that same position as when He died, with His Arms open wide. His life poured out of Him from the injuries He suffered. He did it willingly for us, He took the scourging, the falls under the weight of the cross, the insults, the spit, the crown of thorns, the nails, and the spear to His side. The glory of Christ, the image of God, was on full display that day.

Now we must let His Light shine out of our hearts so others can see God's glory of the gift He gave us: His only begotten Son. *"All this is for your benefit so that the grace that is reaching more and more people may cause thanksgiving to overflow to the glory of God."* **2 Corinthians. 4:15** When Jesus was nailed and raised on the cross, it was the final triumph as He continues to draw all people to Him. Without the shedding of blood there is no forgiveness of sin. We must develop *unshakable faith* and stand firm until the end—no matter what we face. Then we can take that Golden Walk into paradise and praise Him for eternity.

No Sinking Feeling

Many years ago, I took my (then newlywed) wife Irma on a cruise so she could experience the joy of snorkeling. We had one small problem - she did not know how to swim. I should have enrolled her in a swimming school before our cruise.

Oh, that reminds me of a humorous experience we had at the Goldfish Swim School about two weeks ago. It's just something to make you smile:

The Goldfish Swim School

Irma and I went to breakfast yesterday morning in Northwest Austin. We parked our truck near a business called the Goldfish Swim School.

I was being silly and asked Irma, "Do you think they really teach goldfish how to swim?" Irma said, "Whaaat?" I responded, "Probably not, but for sure they teach them how to hold their breath underwater." Irma laughed and just said, "Too funny!"

We had a fabulous breakfast and when we got back to our vehicle, I noticed a young woman who worked there was inside the Goldfish Swim School.

I told Irma I needed to go ask the young lady a question. As I got to the locked door, she hurried to open it and asked me to come in. I told her I just wanted to ask her a question. Unbeknownst to Irma, I told the young lady my wife had a very serious question as I pointed to Irma inside the truck. I stayed completely poker faced and said, ***"She wants to know if you really teach goldfish how to swim."*** Her reaction was priceless as she trampled around while thinking about her response. I could tell she was flabbergasted. She blurted out, "NO! We teach children how to swim!" My face had to practice self-control although my insides were quivering hysterically with laughter, I said, "Ohhh, okaaay, thank you. Merry Christmas!"

As we pulled away from the parking spot, the young lady glared at us and we saw her shaking her head in disbelief. Not only did we have the best time at breakfast, but the dessert of laughter was also refreshing. It's the simple things in life. Last night we still chuckled to tears as we relived the "goldfish moment" at bedtime wondering how that young lady's day went.

A cheerful heart is good medicine!

Meanwhile back on our cruise . . . We were near Cheeseburger Reef in Grand Cayman on a pontoon boat. I was determined to get Irma into the water. After all, she was on the edge of the boat wearing a life jacket, face mask and snorkel in place . . . All she needed was to take the plunge. I went into the water first and coaxed her into getting into the water using the ladder at the rear of the boat.

When she got into the water, she panicked as the life vest crept up and kept her awkwardly afloat. Her necked stretched above the life vest in the same manner a turtle stretches its neck to eat the top off some tall grass. I had to reassure her she would not sink as I held her close to me. The boat guide offered us a round lifesaver that had a rope attached to it. Irma was able to hold on to the lifesaver and look through the center to see a beautiful, underwater world with brightly-colored exotic fish and coral.

The guide was kind enough to pull the long rope as he swam in front of us. I swam next to Irma giving her additional security with my arm around her waist. We ended up snorkeling to a distance of about 100 yards away from the boat. Our snorkeling adventure ended well because she grabbed on to the lifesaver and did not let go.

Prior to meeting Irma, I was drowning in alcohol and sinking deeper into darkness. I knew my life was wrong but I did not know how to fix it. I called out to the Lord one Sunday morning in New York City at St. Patrick's Cathedral. You can read about this in **Broken Walk: Searching for Wisdom.**

For the remainder of my life, I vow to write in gratitude to God for saving my life and placing me on the Path to Peace. The three Christian books I have written are to bring Glory to God alone - Soli Deo Gloria! I want others with a similar upbringing as mine to know Jesus is the only way to the Father. I want to share how I was able to overcome alcohol addiction and being stuck in a world of darkness and regret. I also want to share my full joy of becoming a Child of the King. I started life as a child in a little church and had Big Faith. Now I am advanced in age and glad to have my Biggest Faith yet.

The remainder of my life is to bring glory to God through my writing. I am on my way to Heaven and want to tell others about how my life has changed after

I accepted Jesus as my ***Lifesavior***. I have double vision as my eyes seem to look in two directions at the same time as I look back to the past and into my future. I look back at my past with gratitude as I have now forgiven myself and others. As I look to the future, I am excited and in awe of my eternal life in Heaven.

The conclusion of this short story comes with the following image. Picture this: Our Creator threw down from Heaven a lifesaver named Jesus to us. (A lifesaver has a rope attached to it to pull a drowning person out of the water.) That same Lifesaver is seated at the right Hand of the Father and is pulling us all the way into Heaven.

Jesus said it: **"And I, when I am lifted up from the earth, will draw all people to myself." John 12:32**

Grab on to our Lifesavior and enjoy the ride into Heaven. Will you join me In Heaven?

The Titanic

The night the Titanic sank in 1912 on April 14th, 1,528 people went from the sinking ship into the frigid waters. John Harper was there to save as many as he could, physically and spiritually. After putting his only daughter on a lifeboat, he began swimming frantically to help as many people as he could in the freezing water. Reverend Harper was determined to lead everyone he could to accept Jesus as Lord and Savior before the victims froze to death or drowned, including up to his death.

Pastor Harper swam up to one young man who was able to get on top of a piece of floating debris. Reverend Harper asked him as he was struggling between breaths, "Are you saved?" The young man's response was that he had not accepted Jesus as Lord.

Reverend Harper then tried to lead him to Christ only to have the young man, who was going into shock from hypothermia, reply in a negative manner. John Harper then took off his life jacket and threw it to the young man. He blurted, "Here then, you need this more than I do!" as the pastor swam away to help other people.

A few minutes later Harper swam back to the young man and this time, he succeeded in leading him to salvation. Of the 1,528 people that went into the water that night, only six were rescued by the lifeboats. One of them was this young man that was floating on the debris.

It is interesting to note, that when they posted the list in the Cunard Cruise line office in New York later that day, there were only two categories: Lost and Saved. This is exactly how God sees humanity from Heaven right now.

Four years later, at a survivors meeting, a young man stood up and in tears recounted how John Harper had led him to Christ. He also told everyone how Reverend Harper had tried to swim back to help other people, but because of the intense cold, he soon became too weak to swim. His last words before going under in the frigid, icy waters were *"Believe on the name of the Lord Jesus and you will be saved."*

Does Hollywood include this story or remember this man? Of course not!!! Hollywood has a different agenda than glorifying God. This servant of God, John Harper, did everything he could to help others until his final breath – Just like Jesus.

While other cowardly men were trying to buy their way onto the lifeboats (designated for children and women) to save their selfish life, John Harper gave up his life so that others could be saved. Pastor Harper recognized the urgency required in this helpless situation. When, *not if*, I get to Heaven, I hope to talk with John Harper so I can thank this hero. He is the quintessential example of fulfilling the scripture below.

"This is how we know what love is: Jesus Christ laid down his life for us. And we ought to lay down our lives for our brothers and sisters."
1 John 3:16

Note: While serving in the Navy I experienced the once-in-a-life-time privilege of swimming in the middle of the Indian Ocean. It was a bright sunny day with dark blue water that was not cold. My ship was not sinking and we were protected from sharks by armed sailors on the Captain's boat nearby. Even in this setting, there were many young sailors from my ship that chose not to dive in that day. This story is featured in **Broken Walk: Searching for Wisdom.**

It is difficult for me to comprehend the chaos and dismay of the Titanic victims perishing in freezing water as they gasped for air prior to sinking in the dark abyss with no hope. *What a horrible death it must have been for those perishing to watch the luxurious Titanic sink in the vast darkness of an icy grave!* **John Harper was able to get a few of the doomed to Know Peace when there was no peace. He introduced a few of them to the Way when the only way they were destined was down. Through Jesus, Reverend Harper gave some of them eternal Life just before they gasped their last breath.**

Keep in mind, if you are with someone that is dying and unconscious, they can still hear you. Give them the opportunity to accept Jesus by asking them if they believe that God sent Jesus to save us. Ask the person if they believe Jesus died for us and He rose again on the third day. Have the person squeeze your hand if they believe. Say a prayer requesting forgiveness for them. They can hear you all the way until their final breath. I know because my father on his final day had been in a coma all day. That night, as he struggled during his last breaths, I leaned into him and told him, "Dad, jump into Jesus arms!" My father suddenly reached out and took three long breaths and he was gone. My father's soul had departed as I lowered his upper torso back onto his pillow. He was instantly absent from his body and present with the Lord. Alleluia!

Thank you, Jesus for taking my father Home. It was the most peaceful moment in my life as it was the closest, I have ever been to Jesus who visited my father's room that night. I'll see you soon, dad.

Salvation Station lesson # 4 . . . God the Father sent His Son as our LifeSavior – grab on to Jesus and don't let go.

Recommended song to *tune you into the wisdom* about the message in this chapter is: **Born Again** by NewsBoys. It can be found on YouTube with lyrics.

CHAPTER 5

TALKING ON EGGSHELLS

"The mouths of the righteous utter wisdom, and their tongues speak what is just."

Psalms 37:30

Definition for talking on eggshells: To be extremely careful when talking to someone in order to not upset them.

We need to stop 'talking on eggshells' and be bold with any chance we get to testify - no matter who it is we are talking to. Many Christ followers make the mistake of staying quiet and 'going along just to get along.' Shutting up is the last thing believers should do because if there are no words, there is no faith that comes from hearing and consequently leads to no salvations.

We have to roar like a lion when speaking about our Faith. Did you know that the ground shakes when a lion roars? The lion lets everyone around him know that he is the king of the jungle. Be like a lion and roar when you are telling others about the King of kings of the universal jungle. Speak with confidence when sharing the Truth of the Good news. At the end of the book of Matthew, Jesus gave the command to his disciples to 'go make disciples' of all nations. As followers of Christ, we cannot be effective if we hold back when sharing our faith. *Boldness is a byproduct of the Holy Spirit*; use it with confidence and enthusiasm.

How can we engage without being seen as a zealot? Answer: They don't care when they tell you sin is right. It is better to speak up about the Truth than to be afraid to offend them. Trust me, many are looking to be offended and then blame you for *your difference of their opinion.* The focus has to be on what's right, not who's right.

How do we let them know you do not agree with what they are saying? You first listen, then let them know you heard it. Then you ask them to listen while you tell them why you disagree. Our biggest communication problem is . . . *we listen to respond rather than listening to understand.*

Remember, if you are following the law of the land and living a life that brings Glory to God, their dislike or opinion of how you live does not give them the right to disrespect you. After all, who are you trying to please, God or man?

When do you speak up? What did Jesus do? Jesus stayed in a close relationship with God our Father. He knew that He was on earth to glorify the Father. We have His example to follow. It is not easy, but I know many of us are dismayed with the current condition of our world where wrong is right and everything is permissible. When does it stop? How do we get our beloved country healed from spuddle? **Note: What does spuddle mean?** *Noun spuddle (plural spuddles) A mess or confusion where there is lots of activity but nothing gets accomplished* . We don't want to be a nation led by spuddlers that are content with spuddly behavior that does not deal with the task at hand.

Always Pray First

Just today my posting on Facebook read, "**Jesus came as the Lamb of God to die for our sins. And He is returning as the Lion of Judah to take us home!**"

Within minutes, the comment I received from a spuddler was, *"Trump already said he's the lion of Judah. You need Jesus to find another moniker. Trump trademarked "Lion of Judah." You can preorder hat and T-shirts."* It was this person's attempt to derail my posting into a political engagement for his entertainment. I have almost 4,000 followers on Facebook.

My first reaction was to delete the comment, my second was to attack with a counter comment. After prayer, I responded, *"This posting is focused on the Lion of Judah as mentioned in Revelation 5:5. No one else can compare to Him."* This is an example of how I had to turn on my **SKY-FI** and connect with God through prayer before responding. I <u>did not</u> get any more comments from this person on this posting and did receive several likes on my response.

It begins with prayer so God can help us find the right words that glorify Him. We must stay centered with God so He can open the windows to Heaven and give us insight and Wisdom when speaking. In **2 Chronicles 7:14** it says, *"**if My people, who are called by My name, will humble themselves and pray and seek My face and turn from their wicked ways, then I will hear from heaven, and I will forgive their sin and heal their land**."*

Prayer is powerful . . . The power of prayer is not in the one saying it. The power of prayer activates and increases Faith in the one who is hearing it. *"**Consequently, faith comes from hearing the message, and the message is heard through the word about Christ."* Romans 10:17 NIV**

SKY-FI (a.k.a. prayer) is our instant connection to plug into the power of Heaven. It's our open line to the throne - it is our link between God's will and what **He wants accomplished on earth as it is in Heaven.** God is available 24/7/365, He will not put you on hold or say I have to call you back with the excuse of having a poor connection.

This reminds me of a phone call I received while I was on assignment in Washington DC around twenty years ago. It was an early morning call from a young man who lives in west Texas. The day before I had loaned him my prized possession (1997 Buick Riviera) because he was under 25 and was too young to rent a car for a job interview that was out of town. When I answered his phone call he blurted, "I hit a deer with your car." My brain went into shock and I had to quickly muzzle my mouth. I mumbled, "I need to call you back." As soon as I hung up, my angry reaction caused me to jump up and down as I told Irma what had happened. She looked at me and asked, "Did he get hurt?" It surprised me when I told her, "I don't know." I went on to tell her that I had to hang up before I said anything that was hurtful.

After a minute or so, I composed myself enough to call him back. I began my conversation with him by asking if he "had a buck on him." I'm sure glad God doesn't hang up on us and say "I need to call you back" when we really need His Ear. To put some closure on this story, he did not get hurt and we remain *deer* friends with him and his wife Felicia. Their five kids call us grandma and grandpa Tweet. His nickname is Billy Deer or sometimes I call him Venado.

While I am still off the main subject of this chapter, I want to share a little humor on the importance of using commas correctly.

I saw a sign that said: Duck, Eggs!
And I thought – "that's an unnecessary comma!
Then . . . IT HIT ME!

Most Christians are not using the full power of prayer in our daily lives because we are '*talking on eggshells*' while the darkness of the world screams. Being louder does not make it righter. Be an extension cord from Heaven by connecting to His word and letting people hear about your bold, unfiltered Faith.

Prayer must be our first reaction instead of our last resort in an emergency. Quit acting like you have a miniature magic lamp with a genie inside in your pocket that you can pull out when needed. Prayer is the key that unlocks the door to begin your day and also the 4-digit code to set your bodily security system at night so you can sleep securely. Develop a personal communication line with God that is just as real as if you are talking to your ***Bestest***. Your communication about Him with others should be part of your testimony to give Him all glory. Testimony is so powerful it is used in the same sentence as the blood of the Lamb when referring to defeating Satan. "***They triumphed over him by the blood of the Lamb and by the word of their testimony.***" **Revelation 12:11**

The second part to go along with prayer is praise. Being able to tell others about how God changed you is a powerful example of praise. Tell others how God has taken you from darkness to light and blessed you with peace. It is important for me to pause here and write about the word *blessed* while I am thinking about it. Being blessed is not about having worldly possessions or accumulated wealth. You are not blessed because you have a toll tag on your Corvette.

Blessed

So, what does it mean to be *blessed*? The word *blessed* Jesus used in the Sermon on the Mount is from the Greek word **_makarios_**, which means to be happy or blissful, but it also means a self-contained happiness. The Greeks called the Island of Cyprus "the happy isle." They believed that because of its geographical location, perfect climate, and fertile soil that anyone who lived on Cyprus had it 'made in the shade'. And the term they associated with the island Cyprus was makarios. They believed everything you needed to be happy was right there in Cyprus.

Since we can't all move to Cyprus, the basis of our happiness has to be independent of where we reside; no matter where we live or where life twists and turns has taken us. We have to bloom regardless of where we are planted, including your work setting. Being blessed is self-contained, meaning that regardless of what is happening to us externally, we can be truly happy internally. We are genuinely *blessed* as followers of Jesus Christ because we know where we are going – Heaven. **Once we fully grasp that we are spiritual beings living in a temporary human body, it gives you the freedom to survive anything in this life.** Being *blessed* is having that unspeakable joy that comes from having Jesus in our hearts. The joy of the Lord is our strength and it keeps us focused on our upcoming eternal blessing.

Telling Others about Jesus

Below is an example of how to tell others about Jesus by using the talent God has given you. My method is through writing while others testify through music.

Below is an example of how to do it through the lyrics in a song that is popular today. Paraphrased from **Let me tell you 'bout my Jesus found in YouTube:**

> He rose from the grave and set me free
> Who would care that much about me?
>
> Who can wipe away the tears
> From broken dreams and wasted years
> And tell the past to disappear? Oh
> **Let me tell you 'bout my Jesus**
>
> And all the wrong turns that you would
> Go and undo if you could
> Who can work it all for your good
> Let me tell you about my Jesus
> His love is strong and His grace is free
> And the good news is I know that He
> Can do for you what He's done for me
> **Let me tell you 'bout my Jesus!**

Listen to the words . . . And let my Jesus change your life. If He did it for me, I know He can do it for you.

Harvest Time

I personally know a couple that has been spreading the gospel through music for more than 51 years. Their life of serving God and telling others the Good News through praise and worship has been remarkable.

Joel and Rose Perales have been singing Southern Gospel music for more than half a century and are continuing strong. They are a couple completely devoted to doing God's work and it is the only job they have ever had. You can find them at www.peralesministries.com. Since churches were shut down in March 2020 due to the plandemic, the Perales have established an on-line ministry that is heard worldwide. Irma and I have been privileged to assist them when they perform at a scheduled event on several occasions. They have become some of our dearest friends.

Joel has written hundreds of songs and it is interesting to hear him give the meaning to the lyrics of a song. My favorite is Harvest Time, written in Spanish by Carlos Cortez and translated into English by Joel Perales.

Before they sing this song, Joel introduces it by telling how the last words of someone who is leaving you with final instructions are so meaningful. In this case the words were coming from Jesus as His last teaching; the setting is found in the Gospel of John, Chapter 21. Some of the disciples had been fishing and Jesus is waiting for them early in the morning on the shore. Jesus prepared breakfast for them and it was the third time He appeared to His disciples after His resurrection from the dead. Below are Jesus final instructions to Peter:

"When they had finished eating, Jesus said to Simon Peter, "Simon son of John, do you love me more than these?" "Yes, Lord," he said, "you know that I love you." Jesus said, "Feed my lambs." Again, Jesus said, "Simon son of John, do you love me?" He answered, "Yes, Lord, you know that I love you." Jesus said, "Take care of my sheep." The third time he said to him, "Simon son of John, do you love me?" Peter was hurt because Jesus asked him the third time, "Do you love me?" He said, "Lord, you know all things; you know that I love you." Jesus said, "Feed my sheep." John 21:15-17

Peter was hurt by this conversation because the Lord asked him three times if he loved Him. This conversation had a two-fold purpose. First to reinstate Peter for his three denials of the Lord and secondly to give Peter a final command about feeding and taking care of His sheep. The Lord was about to leave the earth to take His rightful place in Heaven. He was entrusting Peter to take care of His flock (us) after He was gone. Personally, I had not made this connection about final instructions prior to having it explained by Joel Perales. It gives so much more meaning to the song and increases my urgency to lead others to Christ.

Below are the lyrics to Harvest Time with permission from Joel Perales to use them.

DO YOU LOVE ME, DO YOU TRULY LOVE ME
DO YOU LOVE ME, SINCERELY, DO YOU LOVE ME
TROUBLE TIMES WILL SURE COME
AND WILL TURN YOUR HEART AROUND
HEAVEN AND EARTH WILL PASS AWAY
BUT MY LOVE FOR YOU WILL STAY
DO YOU LOVE ME, DO YOU LOVE ME
DO YOU LOVE ME

CAST YOUR EYES UPON THE HARVEST
MY SON ITS HARVEST TIME
CAN'T YOU SEE THE DAYLIGHT'S FADING
AND SOON COMETH THE NIGHT
WILL YOU HELP ME REAP THE HARVEST
MY SON, THERE'S LITTLE TIME
IF YOU TRULY, TRULY LOVE ME
FEED MY SHEEP, IT'S HARVEST TIME

DO YOU LOVE ME, MY SON, DO YOU LOVE ME
I LOVE YOU LORD, YOU KNOW ALL THINGS
THEN FEED MY LITTLE CHILDREN
THE SHEEP HAVE GONE ASTRAY
BUT IT'S URGENT, YOU MUST GO NOW
DON'T FALTER DON'T DELAY
DO YOU LOVE ME, DO YOU LOVE ME
DO YOU LOVE ME?

The song is published by Roel Publishing Company – BMI. Please take time to listen to it, you will definitely be blessed.

Dakota Rae's Ministry Debut

Contributed by my wife Irma

"But Jesus called the children to him and said, "Let the little children come to me, and do not hinder them, for the kingdom of God belongs to such as these." Luke 18:16

What does a 3-year old have in common with a 72-year old? Especially when grandpa is one of the most talented song writer/musicians ever to be born.

Answer: **Music**, **ministry** and **singing**!

Dakota Rae Perales is destined to be the next great singer to follow in the Perales legacy. She is the daughter of Jonathan and Chardonnay Perales.

During a recent service celebrated at Cathedral of Faith in San Antonio, Joel and Rose Perales were bringing worship in a concert setting. This was a day after Rose's dad celebrated his 95th birthday. Dakota Rae was presented as an unexpected guest singer that morning but she delayed her debut by an unplanned little nap prior to her introduction. Her debut song was anticipated as one of three choices: '**Jesus Loves the Little Children**', or '**The B.I.B.L.E.**', or even '**This Little Light of Mine**'.

Dakota Rae slowly walks up to the microphone with her Nana Rose and 'Honey' (Grandpa Joel). She takes the mic and starts to sing . . . *Twinkle, Twinkle Little Star* . . . Nana says let's sing '**Jesus Loves Me**'. Dakota says she wants to sing **Twinkle, Twinkle Little Star** not minding everyone else. She starts out: *Twinkle, Twinkle Little Star.* Not quite 3-years old at the time, unbeknownst to this precious little girl, singing her special little song of choice touched someone deeply. It was as if the Holy Spirit prompted Dakota to sing this unplanned song. At the time it seemed sort of out of place. The congregation listened and seemed to fidget awkwardly.

Later that afternoon, after the service at the church, there was a meet-and-greet gathering. As testimonies were shared, a young woman at the event let those at the get-together know her mother had just passed away a few days earlier in the week. She shared that when Dakota sang Twinkle, Twinkle Little Star, it made her start crying. The young woman had not been able to cry since her mom's passing even though she knew her mother had transitioned into her heavenly eternity. Dakota's anointed song from her little voice instantly brought tears, peace, and comfort to a mourning daughter. It reassured her that her mom was in Heaven and doing well.

That first moment of being able to shed tears of grief during that service helped her with her grieving process.

A little child of God, starting her little ministry, not only of music and singing, but of ministering while guided by the Holy Spirit. '*Let the little children come to me, and do not hinder them, for the kingdom of God belongs to such as these.*'

Glory to God! My prayer is that thousands more are touched by Dakota's future singing. May she continue the legacy her grandparents have established over the past fifty years.

To God be the Glory!

My Music Before Christ (BC) was Loud and Proud

After I accepted Jesus as Lord and Savior, there was a new song in my heart. The song fits right in with the beating of my heart. Did you know your heart beats about 100,000 times per day or 36,500,000 per year? Thinking about all those heart beats suddenly makes me feel more tired than I really am.

As a young man I tried to influence the world with the music I listened to: Motown, Beatles, Three Dog Night, Santana, Chicago, and so forth. *The louder, the better!* Now as a "seasoned, wiser man," I do not listen to loud music, but I hear a continuous song in my heart with no lyrics. It has calmed my overall well-being and provides nourishment to my soul.

Proverbs 9:3 tells how Wisdom called out from the highest point in the city. **"Leave your simple (means foolish) ways and you will live; walk in the way of insight" Proverbs: 9:6**. Wisdom has taught me to listen to the music that is mostly about Jesus. This music makes me dance to the beat of a different Drummer; The One who is way better than Ringo Starr. That reminds me of a comment John Lennon made when asked if Ringo was the greatest drummer in the world. John quickly responded, *"He is not even the best drummer in the Beatles!"*

You will not hear loud music blasting from my vehicles anymore. My changed heart plays a continuous song without my knowledge of the lyrics. Even though the rhythm of my heart changes with exertion or excitement, the silent lyrics always resonate love, peace, and joy.

When I sincerely asked Jesus to come into my heart on that crisp November morning, my change was instant. Immediately, a wave of warmth covered me from head to toe, and my heart seemed to be expanded so Jesus could live there. My lungs got unclogged as I breathed in His Life. Having Christ in my heart is like wearing thermal clothing when it is cold outside. It is like your heart is receiving a constant Heavenly hug from Jesus. My salvation has fueled me with an urgency to speak and write about Jesus at any opportunity. One of my cousins calls me a super Jesus Follower with a pen – I am eternally grateful to receive such a moniker because I know my past and also know I will not return to it.

I have wondered if a heart physically changes when someone receives salvation. If my heart could talk, would it have told you my addiction to alcohol was now gone? Would feelings of anger, resentment, hatred, jealousy, plotting revenge, unforgiveness, loneliness, and selfishness put in a change of address? Could you see a sign on my heart that reads, Next stop – Heaven! I welcome that last beat from my heart because when that stop finally comes, I will be absent from this grandad bod and be present with the Lord. Glory!!!

Does a heart make a noise when it changes? Is there a sound when it transforms from stone to freshly plowed ground? Does the blood flow sound like a babbling brook? Would the sound you hear resemble a giggle from a young child? Does a heart sing when your soul is forgiven? Is there a sweet sound like a bird's song as it awaits the sunrise?

Perhaps the sound is like the delicate ping from the triangle during a symphony. Once you get set free, your heart will never be the same. My heart now sings perpetual tunes without words and will never stop praising.

Ask Jesus to come into your heart so you can go into the world and praise with the song your heart is longing to sing. The melody that comes from your heart will come out as a smile as bright as the sun. You can then start the day with praise and end your day with thanksgiving. May God guide you as you *tune into Wisdom*! That way you can walk with confidence and speak with boldness about how God changed you. Turn up the volume and stop '*talking on eggshells*' about your Faith and where you are going.

Salvation Station lesson # 5 Quit talking on eggshells when telling others of the Good News. Roar like a lion because the word of our testimony and changed behavior glorifies God.

Recommended song to *tune you into the wisdom* about the message in this chapter is: **Raise A Hallelujah** by Bethel Music. You can find it with lyrics on YouTube.

CHAPTER 6

ON PURPOSE

"In him (Jesus) was life, and that Life was the light of all mankind."
John 1:4

God sent His only begotten son from Heaven to Earth *on purpose*. Jesus completed His work on Earth *on purpose*.

Have you ever wondered, "What is my purpose in life? If you haven't, you should.

"The meaning of life is to find your gift ... the <u>purpose</u> of life is to give it away." **Pablo Picasso**

Let's look at this quote in a different manner as it relates to Jesus. The meaning of His Life was to be our gift; the <u>purpose</u> of His Life was to give it away. Christ is our perfect Gift because God loved us so much, He gave us His only begotten Son. Jesus knew His *purpose* in life when He gave it **all** away for us on the Cross.

It was all done on purpose: *"For the bread of God is the bread that comes down from heaven and gives life to the world."* Today is the time for you to understand your purpose and celebrate the rest of your life in a special way. It begins by accepting Jesus as your Lord and Savior.

This must be done <u>on purpose</u>. **Accept the Gift** of Christ as your Lord and Savior. Be part of the chosen people, God's special possession, so we can praise Him because He has taken us out of the darkness and into His wonderful light. It's the best gift you will ever receive and then do something else <u>on purpose</u>: **Give the Gift away** by sharing Him with others.

The Kingdom of God is near!

The meaning of Jesus life was to be our gift from God, His life mission was to give it away. His overall *purpose* was to glorify God. Jesus fulfilled His *purpose* when He gave it all away at the Cross. He proclaimed His ministry on earth when He quoted the prophet Isaiah early in His ministry. *"**The Spirit of the Lord is on me, because he has anointed me to proclaim good news to the poor. He has sent me to proclaim freedom for the prisoners and recovery of sight for the blind, to set the oppressed free, to proclaim the year of the Lord's favor.**"* **Luke 4: 18-19** Those who were in the synagogue were *amazed at the gracious words that came from His lips.*

Jesus knew that His mission in His human life was to give his life away. Did He know how much He would suffer? Of course, He was the Son of God. He knew His blood had to be shed to take away the sin of the world. In the Garden of Gethsemane, He told His disciples that His soul was overwhelmed with sorrow to the point of death and His sweat was like drops of blood to the ground. He asked God in prayer, *"**Father, if you are willing, take this cup from me; yet not my will but yours be done.**"* **Luke 22:42**

Jesus knew He would be whipped, punched, crowned with thorns, nailed to the cross, spit on, stripped of his dignity, and mocked but **He did it anyway**. He even asked God to *"forgive them for they know not what they do."* He died nailed to the cross with spit on His face as His Hands were immobilized by the nails and He could not wipe it off. *He was like a rose, trampled on the ground, He took the fall, and thought of us, above all.*

So, next time you feel fear, abandonment, loneliness, depression, pain, and illness call on Him because He has experienced all of our human emotions.

Most of all, He is the only person to come back to life after He had been dead and buried in a grave. His body was wrapped and the grave was sealed for three days. If you are reading this you haven't died yet, *but you will*. And since you will, don't you need the help of someone who knows the way out? Hope you are *tuned* into Jesus by this point in this reading.

God has given us a new birth into everlasting life through the resurrection of Jesus. He fulfilled another promise when he said, *"And I, when I am lifted from this earth, will draw all people to myself."* **John 12:32** This provides The Way for us to have life that cannot be destroyed!

Given a Life Sentence

It is like a modified oxymoron when you receive a 'life sentence' as your punishment. A life sentence is a prison term that typically lasts for one's lifetime. *Isn't that really a death sentence?*

I want to explore the term 'life sentence' in both the physical and spiritual realm. In 2013, I was living a death sentence as my heart was in poor condition. Physically I could do no strenuous work, get too emotional or forget to take my medication. I was taking a stroll towards the grave and about to take a *dirt nap*. (*Dirt nap* is slang for death, I learned this from my Tia Weenie)

Exhaustion and worry consumed me with thoughts of when a stroke would hit or my heart would give out. My irregular heartbeat would sometimes get stuck on full steam ahead; this increased my chances of suffering a stroke dramatically. This required visits to the ER to get my heart back to normal rhythm. After a few months of suffering with this, I asked my cardiologist, "how fast of a heart rate is too fast?" and "how long of a period of an increased heart rate is too long?" His response was, "As long as you can take it!" I told him I cannot live this way. (*Watch your words, they may come true*) He informed me of a new procedure called an ablation which could only be performed by a Medical Doctor of Cardiac Electrophysiology. Long story short, here's a fast forward from **Broken Walk: Searching For Wisdom** to the recovery room:

"After a three-hour heart ablation, I woke up in recovery with 10-12 other patients that had just come out of surgery. My mind went into 'test mode' for determining if I had suffered a stroke. I stuck out my tongue and moved it from right to left. If my tongue remained limp, I failed the test if it was hanging to one side. This would mean I was stroked out. As my tongue slid into my mouth, I smiled and thanked God out loud. A nurse said, "He's not supposed to be awake yet!" My next test was to perform a memory check conducted by Dr. Roo (me). This self-test was to check my brain as I excavated in the caverns of my memory. As I remembered Christmas in 1958, I saw my cousin Mariam receiving a toy monkey with cymbals and I shouted, "Yes!" As I raised my right arm in praise, a nurse reprimanded me and told me to 'Be still!' Hmmm ... I've heard those words before. God had brought me back from the dead."

On the physical side, I am feeling great nine years after the ablation. I occasionally do silly things like going into a room in the house and not remembering why. My most recent older man blunder was to place my dark coffee cup with the bottom up (it was dark) while the Keurig did its job. Don't tell Irma. LOL

On the spiritual side before I was *born again,* I was a walking, clueless zombie. *I was like a blind man wearing sunglasses in a dark room looking for a black cat that was not there!* **"A fool walks in darkness while a wise man has eyes in his head."** Let me explain this scripture found in Ecclesiastes 2:14. I struggled with this scripture because I was trying to figure it out from the physical rather than spiritual sense. In my opinion, it means once you receive salvation, even if you become physically blind you still have <u>vision</u> of where you are going, that is, Heaven.

On November 13, 1999, my life changed! I was given an eternal *life sentence* by Jesus Christ. I am a new creation and now, **"I have been crucified with Christ and I no longer live, but Christ lives in me." Galatians 2:20 <u>So, read this part closely, if I no longer live does that mean I received a death sentence?</u>** ABSOLUTELY NOT!!! It is another modified oxymoron in the spiritual realm as I have been given life abundantly. I have never had more freedom! Now I pray that as a 'prisoner for the Lord' (Ephesians 4:1) that I am able to live a life worthy of the calling I have received. Thank you, Jesus!

When I sincerely asked Jesus to come into my heart on that crisp November morning, my change was instant. Immediately, a wave of warmth covered me from head to toe and my blood danced in my veins. My lungs got unclogged as I breathed in Life. A 100-pound weight was taken off my shoulders.

I have wondered if a heart physically changes when you receive salvation. The following is taken in part from <u>Broken Walk: Searching For Wisdom</u>.

"If my heart could talk, would it tell you my addiction to alcohol is gone? Would feelings of anger, resentment, hatred, jealousy, plotting revenge, unforgiveness, loneliness, and selfishness no longer be there?

Does a heart make a noise when it changes? Is there a sound when it transforms from stone to freshly plowed ground? Does the blood flow sound like a babbling brook? Once you get set free, your heart will never be the same. My heart now sings perpetual tunes without words and will never stop praising."

Jesus gave me a Life Sentence … so now I will spend the rest of my life in solitary confinement serving Him only. ***"As a prisoner for the Lord, then, I urge you to live a life worthy of the calling you have received. Be completely humble and gentle; bearing with one another in love. Make every effort to keep the unity of the Spirit through the bond of peace. There is one body and one Spirit, just as you were called to one hope when you were called; one Lord, one Faith, one baptism; one God and Father of all, who is over all and through all and in all." Ephesians 4:1-6***

Are you ready to receive your life sentence? Pinky did, see below.

God Always Has A Better Plan – *O.P.T.B.E.G.*

O.P.T.B.E.G. – what does that mean? It stands for <u>o</u>rdinary <u>p</u>eople <u>t</u>ouched by <u>e</u>xtraordinary <u>G</u>od. Most of us are fairly ordinary, we wake up with bedhead, try to keep up with email messages, and attempt to burn off more calories than what we consume. God touches ordinary people like me and you to further His Kingdom. He used two ordinary midwives to save the life of Moses (Exodus 1:17) and some ordinary fishermen became Jesus' first round draft picks. (Matthew 4:21).

Let me introduce you to Pinky to demonstrate the power of our extraordinary God.

He was not your typical looking Mexican-American as he sported red hair and red freckles when he was born in 1947. His nickname became Pinky because when he was an infant, he would cry so hard that he turned completely pink when forcefully requesting attention or feeding. His maternal grandparents adopted Pinky at the age of two due to the neglect Pinky received from his biological mother. It was the best thing for Pinky as he was raised as a PK (Pastor's Kid) where he learned about faith and trusting God. His grandmother was strict and kept a tight rein on Pinky and his younger sisters. They lived in humble conditions but God always provided what they needed.

Around the time of John F. Kennedy's assassination in 1963, their family moved to Sterling, Colorado. It was and still is a small town near the Nebraska/Colorado border. Pinky was now 16 years old and enjoying the joys of youth. He liked hanging around with his friends and asked for permission to stay overnight at a friend's house. His grandmother was reluctant but agreed as she verbally placed him in God's hands. Pinky was a typical teenager and said, "You're always trying to scare me, nothing is going to happen!' as he went out the front door. She told Pinky he needed to be at church for the 10 am Sunday service.

Later that evening, his friend Paul told Pinky they were going to a party. Pinky had been somewhat sheltered and never had smoked or drank alcohol. At the party, Pinky was thirsty and had several glassfuls of punch. He did not know the punch had been spiked and did not remember much about his time at the party. He ended up passing out and Paul took him home and placed him on the bunk bed fully clothed. Pinky woke up on Sunday morning about 9:40 am with the worst headache he had ever had. (little did he know, he was soon going to feel a headache way worse than that) He jumped out of bed and raked a comb across his head. He smeared toothpaste on his teeth with his finger and yelled to Paul they had to leave for church NOW.

They jumped into Paul's two-door 1952 Chevrolet and sped to church. Going 80 miles per hour, Paul lost control of the car and went into a 10-foot dry canal embankment. The collision caused Pinky to fly through the front window as the rearview mirror ripped the side of his face. His body slammed into the side of the canal but he did not lose consciousness. He heard the medical attendants discussing how they were going to bring him up on the stretcher. Due to the shock and adrenaline, Pinky was able to walk out of the embankment to meet the ambulance drivers at the top of the canal. Somehow, he was able to do this with two broken arms, two broken legs, and a face that was bleeding profusely. Paul did not get ejected from the car as the steering wheel blocked him and kept him in the car.

Later in the hospital, Pinky learned he had a fractured skull, three cracked ribs, and internal bleeding to go with his broken arms and legs. The lacerations he suffered required 65 (double stitched) sutures and required skin grafting later. He heard his grandmother pleading to God to spare him as Pinky was their gift from God. He remembers teetering on the brink of death and had thoughts of going to hell. When his grandfather heard the doctor's report that Pinky might not survive, he prayed for a second opinion from our Master Physician. Pinky felt his grandfather's hand on his chest and begging the Holy Spirit to flow through his grandson's broken body. Instantly, Pinky felt a warm calmness that flowed through him. There was warmth that concentrated and remained in the spots that were most injured. Miraculously, his broken bones were mended and the internal bleeding stopped. *That same power that rose Jesus from the dead, healed Pinky from dying that day.* Pinky wanted to get up and leave but his eyes were still shut from the swelling and he still had a large knot on his forehead. He remained under observation in the hospital for a couple of days and walked out under the power of the Holy Spirit.

Pinky never touched a drink of alcohol after this experience and later learned alcoholism was in his genes through his biological father. Pinky's real name is John Martinez who is now living in retirement with his wife

Lorraine in Spring Hill, Tennessee. John went full time into Ministry and became an Ordained Minister. He has been involved doing God's work all his life. He lived many years in San Jose California and lead many hard-core gang members to follow Christ as the Director of Christian Teen Challenge, and later as Executive Director of Teen Challenge. He is just an ordinary person touched by extraordinary God.

A Cord of Three Strands

In this next story you will read about a couple that was searching for purpose after experiencing the struggles that divorced couples often face. God had a plan for them and with finding each other they found their *purpose*. A marriage should be like an Oreo cookie. It is one cookie made of three parts. The two outside parts represent the husband and wife and the cream in the middle represents God. Both outside parts need to stay connected to the middle (God) for a marriage to remain intact. ***"Though one may be overpowered, two can defend themselves. A cord of three strands is not quickly broken."*** **Ecclesiastes 4:12**

Tommy Bedolla was born in Willcox AZ in 1950, he was the youngest of 14 children of Librada and Marcos Bedolla. Tommy still wonders how his parents were able to provide for all their needs because they never lacked for anything. His parents were raised Catholic so they passed on their beliefs to their children. His mom seemed to be more dedicated to going to Catholic church than his father. However, she was touched when she heard the anointed praise and worship music from the Spanish Assembly of God in Willcox.

When she decided to leave Catholicism, it caused quite a stir in the family. There were more family members that opposed it than those in the family that welcomed it. There at the Assembly of God she was *born again* when she asked Jesus Christ to be her Lord and Savior. She later joined the Anglo Assembly of God in Willcox and was a member there until her passing at the age of 98. Tommy's father also gave his life to the Lord at the Assembly of God Church because of his Mom's persistent prayer for him.

When Tommy's mother took him to church, he visually experienced and heard the presence of God in a powerful way. He witnessed the church being alive through the preaching of the Word, Praise and Worship, people being saved, filled with the Holy Spirit, speaking in tongues, instant healings taking place and prophesying. *God really moved*. People would gather around the altar until the 'Spirit fell' and remained sometimes past midnight. Tommy was about 9 or 10 years old when he first attended one of those services filled with the strong presence of the Lord. He was touched as a young boy during a service. He was in the back with his mom and played on the cement floor, as there was no carpeting in those days. Suddenly a cloud came over him that engulfed him and filled him with peace. It was so special he did not want to leave. Tommy never told anyone about it because he thought people would think he 'was losing touch with reality.' As those youthful years sped by, Tommy did not fully commit to Christ even though he was regularly going to church and seeing the move of God.

During high school, Tommy slowly drifted away from God. He was never a bad kid as he studied hard and his report card was full of A's. As a result, he received a scholarship to Cochise College where he majored in aviation. He was a topnotch student and later was selected to represent his class at the Federal Aviation Administration to see if the professors had taught them correctly. He graduated with honors and received an AA degree in Aviation. Even though Tommy was an excellent student, he always felt an emptiness in his heart while at school. The *void* in the soul is deep and wide without God. Tommy recalls his father once telling him, 'your soul is so big that only God can fill it.'

After graduating from college, he worked at the nearby Army base. His job was to ensure the aircraft used by pilots that were being trained was combat ready for Vietnam. Like most young men he enjoyed socializing with his co-workers and friends. During this period in his life, he stopped going to church and God was no longer a part of his life.

Mother's prayers

Sometimes after drinking with his buddies, he would come home, slightly drunk and proceed to serenade his mother at the foot of her bed. He loved playing the guitar and was already quite talented. Many of his siblings were musicians, so music was always in his blood. His mother did not condemn him for drinking and would enjoy his music until he quieted down. She would then pray for him and Tommy listened to her as the effects of alcohol wore off. She prayed for him, in English, Spanish, and in Tongues. (*This gift is real*). No one can convince Tommy it is not. He heard it and felt the Lord's power as she prayed. In Tommy's words *"One thing I know you can't escape is the prayers of a spirit-filled mom."*

Shortly after this time in his life, he married for the first time and had two children, a boy, and a girl but it ended in a divorce. The lengthy divorce proceedings placed Tommy at the lowest point in his life. He turned to his best friend, his mother who was his everything. He was her 'consentido' as he was her youngest child. He talked to his mom and she gave him the best advice ever by saying, "SON, You need Jesus!" When she said that, for the first time he heard JESUS. Not just in his head, but all the way into his heart and soul.

A few days later his brother Ralph came to see Tommy. This time Ralph was different and Tommy asked, "What's up with you?" Ralph told him his life had been changed as he had given his life to Jesus. *WOW, this is exactly what Tommy longed for.*

A few days later, Tommy went home from his new job that he had recently changed to. He was now working at the electric power plant and was a control room operator. Little did Tommy know his life was about to change because of receiving that *same power* that raised Jesus from the dead. He knelt in the living room and raised his hands and called out to God. "I NEED YOU!" Hallelujah! ***"Everyone who calls upon the Name of the Lord will be saved!"*** ***Romans 10:13*** God heard him as he felt a change from within, it was as if electricity was dancing in his veins. That was the day of his salvation as he received grace and was *reborn* that day. The void was now filled as Tommy was now anchored to the Savior he had drifted from over the years.

He felt compelled to tell someone about his born again experience so he called his brother Rick who was a minister. He pastored a church called

The Jesus Chapel. He was so happy as he had been praying for Tommy also and had also supported him all through his divorce and custody battle. Rick invited Tommy to come to church the following Sunday. As Tommy approached the church he could hear people were praising God. They were singing, *Thy Loving Kindness is Better than Life*. The congregation was all in harmony and it sounded like an Angelic choir. When Tommy opened the door, he thought 'Oh My!' He again saw the same cloud he had experienced as a boy was there. As the cloud engulfed him again. he could not hold back his tears. His brother called Tommy forward and asked if he wanted to be filled with the Holy Spirit. There was no way he could resist. The cloud was the Holy Spirit all over him and now THE COMFORTER wanted to come inside and fill him . . . and HE did. **Hallelujah**!

The divorce mentioned earlier, was taken care of by the Lord and Tommy was awarded custody of his son. His little girl was awarded to her mother, which is another story for another time. Tommy helped his brother Rick with the Jesus Chapel and shortly after began singing for the Lord. Tommy and Rick both loved music and formed a little group that included both of them, Nat, and Rick's sons. Later on, the *Love of his life*, Rita would also sing with some of them. **Note:** *Tommy affectionately calls Rita, His Rib. You have to understand Tommy's humor is a reference to Adam and Eve.*

Tommy ended up raising his son by himself for about 7 years. He did receive some help from his mom and sisters at times but managed well on his own. Tommy was still young and needed a woman in his life that could be a mother to his son. Tommy went to his brother Rick for prayer as he did not want to make another mistake. He asked the Lord to bring the right person into Tommy's life. As Rick prayed for Tommy, the Spirit of the Lord came over him. Tommy had seen this happen before. With his eyes closed Rick prophesied these words. He said the Lord would bring a woman into Tommy's life that would have a heart of gold and would sing with him.

Guess what? She was a Catholic girl (Rita) with 3 kids who was going through her own trials, but she loved the Lord. They had some different opinions because of their religions but Tommy knew it would work out if he obeyed God - No matter what. Tommy found out you can't put God in a box. He does things His way and He does them right. Rita gave her life to the Lord and has loved Him and served Him ever since. She also sings like an angel. She became Tommy's wife and mother to all their kids. *She can tell her own story.* They have had storms come their way but they have stood on the solid Rock Jesus. The storms and the orchestrator of them have been defeated. **Praise be to God**!

Rita's Story

Rita remembers moving to Willcox, Arizona in 1961 with her parents Andres & Socorro Bracamonte and her four siblings. She recalls going to church on Sundays where they attended Catholic mass. She was the oldest child and around the age of 13, she overheard her parents talking late at night. Her mom and dad thought all of the kids were asleep and their conversation was in private. She heard her dad telling her mother that he would not live much longer as he suffered with many health issues. This included coronary issues, diabetes, high blood pressure and gout to name a few. It was about this time that their family began attending mass every day of the week.

Rita loved the nuns and at that time wanted to become one. While attending catechism at the age 9 or 10, Rita heard a teaching by one of the nuns about sin. She vividly recalls seeing the board used for illustrations with a great big red heart on it as she walked into the classroom. The nuns placed black dots on this heart to represent sin. Rita was really impacted and seriously 'took this to heart' and it *terrified* her. She did not fully understand what sin was but she knew she did not want her heart covered with black dots. She thought, can my heart really get filled with these black dots? Can these black dots clog my heart? What will happen to me if I die, where would I end up? This teaching bothered her for a long time.

Her father passed in 1968, when she was 14. Her father's death made their family feel lonely and vulnerable without him. It was an extremely difficult time for Rita, her younger siblings, and mother. Three years later at the age of 17 Rita got married. This marriage lasted only 5 years and she returned to live with her mother along with her three children in 1976. Times were hard but they managed. Her mother was still a very devout Catholic but by now was a *born again* Catholic.

In 1980 as Rita was walking home (she did not have a car) from work at the gas station, Tommy gave her a ride home. she liked him and thought he was cute . . . *She still thinks he is.* At a later time, she finally mustered enough courage to call him and ask him if he wanted to go to a dance with her. Although she didn't care about the dance, it was her reason to hopefully get to know him better. His response surprised her because he said, "No, I don't do those things anymore." Her next question was to ask why. Tommy asked her if she really wanted to know and Rita said "Yes!" He said he had given his life to the Lord and had given 'all that up' because he was serving the Lord. She did not understand what he was talking about so she asked him to explain.

He asked her if she had a Bible and when she replied yes, he had her open it up to **John 3:16**. He told her to read him the scripture. ***For God so loved the world that he gave his only begotten son, that whosoever believeth in him would not perish, but have everlasting life.*** Rita had never heard those words and she asked Tommy to help her understand.

He went on to tell her about Jesus and who He was and how He came to earth and gave His life so that we could be saved. He told her if she accepted Jesus in her heart, He would be her Father and when she left this world, He would be waiting for her in heaven. She fondly remembers telling him YES, that she wanted to accept Jesus and at the same time felt angry because the priest had never told her this. Actually, the masses were in Latin so they never knew what the priest was saying. That day was the day of Rita's salvation as she accepted Jesus into her heart.

At that very moment she went back to her childhood and remembered those dreaded black dots that she had been taught by the nuns. She was able to give the thoughts of sin that had terrorized her all her life to Jesus. Rita cried and cried and couldn't thank Jesus enough for the gift of salvation. ***Who can wash our sins away? Nothing but the blood of Jesus!***

In 1983 Tommy & Rita married and God blended their two families together. Tommy was raising his son and Rita had her three children so they became the Bedolla bunch.

Tommy and his brothers were all Christians and would minister in churches through music wherever they were called. The group was called the Bedolla Brothers: Rick, Nat, Tommy, and Rick's sons. (Rick was the leader) As time went by, the sons left and Tommy and Rick were left alone. Their practice was held at Tommy & Rita's home. One day Rick asked Rita if she could sing and they had a rehearsal on the spot. He had her sing a song and that is how she became part of the music ministry.

This continued for years until illness and age ended the group. Later on, Tommy and Rita began their own group and called it River Of Life. It consisted of the two of them and two friends. The group stayed together from 1996-2004. Today, it is just the two of them and they still go out and sing when they are called. They have found their *purpose* and they are doing it well.

Rita's favorite thing to say is that *I WAS BORN TO BE BORN AGAIN because I couldn't live in this world otherwise.*

Salvation Station Lesson # 6: God always has a better plan; we just need to connect with God and follow His plan so we can find our purpose.

Recommended song to *tune you into the wisdom* about the message in this chapter is: ***No One Ever Cared For Me like Jesus*** by Edith Tripp, You can find it with lyrics on YouTube.

CHAPTER 7

THE BREAD OF GOD

*"For **the Bread of God** is bread that comes down from heaven and gives life to the world." John 6:33*

Jesus died for us on purpose, it was God's salvation plan for mankind. God planned it so well He even sent Jesus to be born into a little town called Bethlehem to give us eternal life. Did you know that Bethlehem means *house of bread* in Greek and Hebrew?

Why did Jesus say I am the bread of life in John 6:35? This is one of the seven I AM statements Jesus makes about Himself; the other six are listed below as you continue this chapter.

Bread is considered an essential food in all cultures, i.e., a basic dietary item. A person can survive a long time on only bread and water. Bread is such a basic food item that it becomes synonymous for food in general. There are limitless kinds of various forms of bread around the world.

My favorite is the flour tortilla, like the ones my mother made regularly throughout my youth. I also love sourdough bread from Fisherman's Wharf and the rye bread in a Reuben sandwich. Hmmm? Does a person from Aruba eating a Reuben sandwich make him a cannibal? Get it? A person from Aruba is an Aruban. I know that's about as corny as the corned beef in a Reuben Sandwich.

Don't get me started on pastries like those fabulous scones. Those can be made from whatever ingredient your tastebuds yearn for. There were no scones in the *barrio* but I'm thankful for the few I've had in these later years. It makes my imagination smile to think about sinking these choppers into a raspberry, poppyseed, buttermilk-based scone. Of course, it must be bedazzled with coarse sugar, a drizzle of melted butter cream, raspberry sauce, and toasted almond slivers on top. Sounds wonderful, huh? Get your mind out of the bakery – that was just a commercial brought from Heaven. Grab some popcorn or pumpkin seeds; this next teaching will focus on The Bread of God – the One and Only Jesus Christ. As you read this next part, it is a teaching to help tune us into Wisdom to help our unbelief and/or increase our Faith.

The Bread of Life

During Jesus, time on earth, unleavened bread was used as an important part of the Jewish Passover meal. The Jews ate unleavened bread during the Passover feast and then for seven days following as their celebration of the exodus from Egypt. Long before Jesus, the ancient Jews fled slavery in Egypt, their firstborn children were "passed over" and spared from death on the eve of the Exodus. You can read about how Moses established the Passover holiday in **Exodus 13:1-16**. You also may have heard the Bible story of when the Jews were wandering in the desert for 40 years and God rained down "bread from heaven" to sustain the nation. If not, please make time to read about this in **Exodus 16:4**.

The above two references lead to the teaching moment as described in John 6 when Jesus uses the term "bread of life." He had crossed the Sea of Galilee, and the crowd followed Him because they saw the signs (miracles) as He healed the sick. Afterwards He took a break and went up to the mountainside with his disciples. When Jesus looked up and saw a great crowd coming toward Him, He asked Philip if he knew how they were going to feed all these people. Philip responds by saying they don't have enough money to give each of them even the smallest morsel of food. Finally, Andrew (Peter's brother) brings to Jesus a boy who had five small loaves of bread and two fish. With that amount, Jesus miraculously fed the throng with lots of food to spare. After all had been fed, they were able to fill twelve baskets with the pieces of the five barley loaves that were left over. ***Remember, do your own research, and check this story in your Bible in John Chapter 6.***

Note: As an author, I can relate to the small boy with five barley loaves and two fish. My prayer, as I leave Salvation Station at the feet of Jesus, is this simple book will reach thousands after it is blessed by our Lord. My hope is for Salvation Station to reach thousands as faith is increased and decisions are made to follow Christ. It is all for the Glory of God alone as profits from book sales are donated to charity.

After the feeding of thousands, Jesus and His disciples cross back to the other side of Galilee. When the crowd sees that Jesus has left, they followed Him again. Jesus takes this moment to teach them a lesson. He accuses the crowd of ignoring His miraculous signs and implies they are only following Him for the "free meal." Jesus tells them in **John 6:27**, ***"Do not labor for the food that perishes, but for the food that endures to eternal life, which the Son of Man will give to you. For on him God the Father has set his seal."*** In other words, He meant they were so absorbed with the food and the healing of the sick, they were missing out on the fact that their Messiah had come. So, the Jews ask Jesus for a *sign* that He was sent from God. (Duh!!! as if the miraculous feeding of thousands was not enough).

The Jews remind Jesus that God gave them manna during the 40 years their ancestors spent in the desert wandering. Jesus responds by telling them that they need to ask for the true bread from Heaven that gives life. When they ask Jesus for this bread, Jesus stuns the crowd by saying, ***"I am the bread of life; whoever <u>comes</u> to me shall not hunger, and whoever <u>believes</u> in me shall never thirst." John 6:35*** At this the Jews began to voice their unbelief because He said, I am the bread that came down from Heaven. They knew Him as Jesus, the son of Joseph, whose father and mother they knew. They were only seeing Jesus with physical eyes instead of spiritual eyes.

"I am the bread of life" is a phenomenal statement!

First, by equating Himself with bread, *Jesus is proclaiming He is essential for life*. As a young boy, I remember asking my father once, what do prisoners eat in jail? He told me 'only bread and water, you don't want to go there!' I'm thankful I never ate an incarcerated meal.

Second, the life Jesus is referring to is not physical life, but *eternal life*. Jesus is trying to get the Jews to shift their thinking from their physical realm and into the spiritual realm. He is contrasting what He brings as their Messiah is everlasting; while the bread He miraculously created the day before was earthly bread that will perish. He is spiritual bread that brings *eternal life*.

Third, and extra important, Jesus is making another claim to deity. This statement is the first of the "I AM" statements in John's Gospel. The phrase "I AM" is the covenant name of God (Yahweh, or YHWH), revealed to Moses at the burning bush (Exodus 3:14). The phrase speaks of being self-sufficient, which is a characteristic only God possesses. It is also an expression the Jews would have automatically understood to be a claim to deity because they knew of the covenant name of God. They were instantly turned off by the use of I AM and they heard it as blasphemy. In their ears, Jesus was showing great disrespect to God by saying I AM the bread of life.

Fourth, in John 6:35, Jesus declares, "***I am the bread of life. Whoever <u>comes</u> to me will never go hungry, and who ever <u>believes</u> in me will never be thirsty.***" Notice the underlined words "comes" and "believes." This is an invitation for those listening to place their faith in Jesus as the Messiah and Son of God. This invitation to come is found throughout the book of John. <u>Coming to Jesus</u> involves making a choice to forsake the world and follow Him. <u>Believing in Jesus</u> means placing our faith in Him that He is who He says He is. As believers, we hold on to the promises that He will do what He says He will do. He also said, He was going to go prepare a place for us and He would take us there after this life. He is the only one who can take us to the Father; He is the Way, the Truth, and the Life. **That's why I believe totally that Jesus is the bread of life.**

Fifth, there are the words "hungry and thirsty." Again, it must be noted that Jesus isn't talking about alleviating physical hunger and thirst. The key is found in another statement Jesus made, back in His Sermon on the Mount. In **Matthew 5:6**, Jesus says, *"Blessed are those who hunger and thirst for righteousness, for they shall be satisfied."* When Jesus says those who *come* to Him will never **hunger** and those who *believe* in Him will never **thirst**, He is saying He will satisfy our hunger and thirst to be made righteous in the sight of God. That way when the rapture comes, we are able to stand in faith and escape the tribulation like mentioned earlier in chapter 3 of this book.

Now let's connect the dots of faith by turning the book back to Chapter 1 <u>right now</u>. Look at the title of Chapter 1: **The Word Became Flesh**. Then read the opening scripture of Chapter 1: *"In the beginning was the Word, and the Word was with God and the Word was God. He was with God in the beginning. Through Him all things were made; without Him nothing was made that has been made. In Him was life, and that life was the light of all mankind. The light shines in the darkness and darkness has not overcome it." John 1:1-5*

The Word (Jesus) was there at the beginning and was God. *All things* were made from Him including each one of us. He gave us His life by becoming flesh and even though Jesus ascended into Heaven, we are left with His word that remains with the earth forever. *"The grass withers and the flowers fall, but the word of our God endures forever."* **Isaiah 40:8** The Word (Jesus) was with God and the Word was God in the beginning (always was) and will endure forever (always will be).

The *Word (Jesus) became flesh* to shine light on the darkness. We must take in this gift into our darkest part of our mind, heart, and soul because *darkness cannot remain where the Light of Heaven falls.* Let this <u>penetrate</u> so you can have His *Life* in you. He was brought down from Heaven to earth to shine His light and life on mankind.

Our problem is: we are like the people who listened to Jesus' *'I am the bread of life message'*. We tend to hear with fleshly minds rather than comprehending with spiritual ears. Jesus was flesh during his thirty three years on earth, but now Jesus sits at the right Hand of the Father praying that one day we will join Him. He is our mediator that provides our way into Heaven. He is the Door, and . . . by believing in the Word (Jesus) our faith unlocks the entrance. ***"Consequently, faith comes from hearing the message, and the message is heard through the word about Christ."*** **Romans 10:17** Accept this Truth and the Word will set you free. The salvation plan is so simple: God loves us so much He gave us His Son. If we believe in Him and follow Him, we get to go to Heaven.

In our human thoughts, especially when we are trying to comprehend that Jesus walked the earth, we still want proof that He was here some 2,000 plus years ago.

The Holy Stairs (Scala Santa)

A few years ago, Irma and I went to Rome and visited a location that I was determined to see to further connect my faith to something physical that Jesus had touched.

La Scala Santa is one of the most valuable relics of the Christian faith, located in Rome. There are twenty-eight marble steps that lead to the Holy of Holies (Latin: Sancta Sanctorum), the chapel of the popes, located in the Lateran Palace (Italian: Palazzo del Laterano).

HIStory tells us, these are the very stairs which Pontius Pilate walked Jesus Christ down to His judgement.

According to the Holy Scripture, the trial of Jesus was held in Pilate's property (Pretoria) in Jerusalem. After Pilot washed his hands of innocent blood (Matthew 27:24), Pilot had Jesus flogged (whipped) and handed him over to be crucified. Sentenced to death, the son of God dripped blood on the stairs as He walked over the wide marble steps. He was on His way to the cross to pay for our sins.

While Irma and I were visiting the Holy Stairs site, a tour guide told us Emperor Constantine I; had this relic moved to Rome as a gift to his mother Iulia Helena Augusta. She later gifted the Santa Scala to Bishop Sylvester . The Bishop gladly accepted the gifts and ordered the relic to be established in the papal palace.

At the end of the 16ᵗʰ century, Lateran Palace was significantly reconstructed. The Scala Santa acquired its current location. It is also assumed that 4 more steps were added to the original 24 ones. Construction works were carried out in a short time, workers did not dare to desecrate the relic with their feet. The staircase was set out from top to bottom.

By the end of the 19ᵗʰ century, the worship of the Scala Santa or Stairs of Pilate (Latin: Scala Pilati) had reached its peak. Numerous pilgrims flocked to the Lateran Palace on the eve of all the great church holidays. People gathered to walk the way from the foot of the stairs to the Basilica of San Lorenzo (Italian: Cappella di San Lorenzo in Palatio) on their knees reading the appropriate prayers at every step. Finally, they had to cover marble under the wooden blades to prevent it from complete destruction.

All the believers going on the stairs feel privileged when looking at traces of blood from the injuries our Savior suffered from the punishment He received prior to His procession to Calvary. There are slits in the form of a cross on the protective wooden panels to allow the view to the most valuable relics of the Holy Stairs – our Lord's bloodstains.

It caused me to be full of mixed emotions as I went up the stairs on my knees. It was hard to be reverent when my surgically repaired right knee was not cooperating. My remnant of unbelief at that time also whispered "*do you really believe they saved the stairs for 2,000 years? You know that scientifically bloodstains cannot last for more than 2,000 years.*" I was still overcome with sadness and was overwhelmed with gratitude thinking of Jesus leaving His blood on those stairs. It is another reminder that the Word became flesh.

Earning our Way

As a young man that loved to play sports, I remember before a game, the coach or a team member would ask, 'Are you ready?' The canned answer from me or other teammates was always, "I was born ready!" This was the ultimate statement that is full of testosterone, confidence and proclaims your invincibility.

As I thought about this, you really aren't born ready until you are born again. When you become born again in Christ, only then, do we become *really born ready*. You are ready to win the game of eternal life and receive the crown of righteousness. Here's the key to victory to all you youngsters, male and female: "*If you stay ready, you won't have to get ready.*" Then when you see Him come back in the clouds, you'll be ready to fly. As a young man I tried to change the world; as a seasoned, wiser man, I did much better by changing my lifestyle through following Jesus.

Empirical studies on the history of human religion tells us that people seek to earn their way to heaven. This is such a basic human desire because God created us with eternity in mind. The Bible says, **"God has placed [the desire for] eternity in our hearts."** (**Ecclesiastes 3:11**). The Bible also tells us that there is **nothing we can do** to earn our way to heaven because we've all sinned (**Romans 3:23**) and the only thing our sin earns us is death (**Romans 6:23**). There is no one who is righteous in himself (**Romans 3:10**). Our dilemma is we have a desire for eternity we cannot fulfill, no matter what we do. That is where Jesus, *the Bread of God* comes in. He, and **He alone**, can fulfill that desire in our hearts for righteousness. **"For our sake He made him to be sin who knew no sin, so that in Him we might become the righteousness of God" (2 Corinthians 5:21).**

When Christ died on the cross, He took the sins of mankind upon Himself and made atonement for them. When we place our faith in Him, our sins are assigned to Jesus, and His righteousness is bestowed on us. This is sometimes referred to as the *Divine Transaction*. Jesus satisfies our hunger and thirst for righteousness because He is our Bread of God that gives life to the world.

All Honor praise and glory to the Lamb of God!

As a bonus, the seven I Am references in the book of John are as follows:

1. **I am the bread of life. (John 6:35)**
2. **I am the light of the world. (John 8:12)**
3. **I am the gate for the sheep. (John 10:7)**
4. **I am the good shepherd. (John 10:11)**

5. **I am the resurrection and the life. (John 11:25)**
6. **I am the way and the truth and the life. (John 14:6)**
7. **I am the true vine. (John 15:5)**

Each name has a special message, make time to read them and enjoy chewing on each story. By doing so, it will help you *tune into Salvation through faith in Jesus.*

No Blueberries in the Barrio

Then Jesus declared, "I am the bread of life. Whoever comes to me will never go hungry, and whoever believes in me will never be thirsty." **John 6:35**

My prayer today is that the scripture above will be a river flowing to nourish the root system of your heart. Flowing into your soul like those canals I used to swim in that provided much needed water in the Valley of the Sun.

Growing up "south of the tracks" in Phoenix Arizona, I didn't have some of the things that I do now. Just to name a few, there were no blueberries in the barrio. Now I eat them almost every day, mixed in with my yogurt to keep me full of antioxidants and regular (it works for me). These little plump, bluish-purple, small pillows of fruity flavor are incredible. I did not get to eat a bagel with cream cheese until age 24 and sushi swam into my mouth (thank God) at age 39. We did not have pajamas in the hood, however, when you do not have these things, you can't miss something that does not exist in your 'hood.

Please do not think I am looking for sympathy – put down those violins and stop that sad music. We were poor, but trust me, I always had way more than I needed growing up in the barrio. We had an abundance of figs, mulberries, pomegranates, nopales, verdolagas and occasionally pecans. My Tio Pancho knew where the best pecan tree stood on private property. He would climb that tall tree and shake it with all his might while he yelled "Charracate! Charracate!" I'm not sure what that word meant, maybe it was passed down from our Aztec ancestors. The word

"Charracate!" seemed to give him the strength of a chango (orangutan). Unlimited pecans hit us as we stood underneath the tree. We had more pecans than you could shake a tree at.

So, what is my point? I want to fill you in on where I was undernourished in the barrio. I did not get to establish a personal relationship with Jesus until age 47 and my father did not make his decision until he was near the end of his life at age 78.

My father used to tease one of my friends named Arturo. He would call him, "Arturo, pan duro!" It rhymes in Spanish and means, Arthur, hard bread. Arturo would get annoyed and asked me, "Why is your dad always hasseling me?" My father would laugh and finish by saying, "El pan no es duro …duro es no tener pan! (the bread is not hard; it is hard not to have bread). He always reminded us how difficult life was when he had to work in the fields from sunrise to sunset instead of being able to go to school. He told us *'we had it made in the shade.'*

As I was walking one morning on vacation near Camelback Mountain and enjoying my time with God, I heard the words, "El pan no es duro … duro es no tener pan! My paradigm got shifted when I thought about this in the spiritual sense. *The undernourishment I had in the barrio was not getting a full portion of the Bread of Life.* It was evident in my father's words when he received salvation. After I read him the story in John chapter 14, he received just what he needed at that moment. When we got to John 14:6, ***Jesus answered "I am the Way and the Truth and the Life. No one comes to the father except through me.",*** my father looked bewildered and said, "So that's where that comes from!" We had only received crumbs by getting part of the bread most of our lives. Most of our church life we only heard or read ***I am the Way***.

I asked my papa if he wanted to hear more and he said, "Yes!" We continued down the Roman route and he made a personal connection with Jesus as Lord and Savior that day! Alleluia! If you get a chance, read about this in the last chapter of *Barrio Walk: Stepping Into Wisdom*. It is the greatest miracle I have ever experienced up to that point. Please understand when the above happened, I was an inexperienced follower of Christ and I was not sure what to tell my father to lead him to Christ. Only by the assistance from the Holy Spirit and the Word, did everything come together for my father's *day of salvation.*

At age 47, I heard the words in John 6:54: *Jesus said, (spiritually)* **"Whoever eats my flesh and drinks my blood has eternal life, and I will raise them up at the last day."** What an awesome promise! Back in those days when Jesus was walking on our Earth, his words were extremely controversial. He lost many followers because those listening to him only knew of what was being taught in the Law by the Pharisees. Many thought, Jesus was off his rocker when they thought about eating physically from His Flesh and Blood. Some people also stop listening to me when I talk about Jesus being the only way to the Father. I grew up reciting the Apostle's Creed at Our Lady of Fatima and still believe that prayer.

I am heaven bound with a renewed heart *to go with my balding head.* When I decided to follow Christ, he yanked me out of the darkness that was fueled by alcohol for 30 years. He put me on the Path to Peace fully clothed and in my right mind. My mind is now centered, and my heart is finally calm. I no longer have to go to a man to confess my sins, I communicate with Jesus directly and daily. ***There is One God and One Mediator between God and man, the Man Christ Jesus.* 1 Timothy 2:5**

Note: writing about 'to go with my balding head' causes me to share something. Recently, my three year old granddaughter looked at me with amazement when I took off my Phoenix Suns ball cap. She exclaimed, "What happened to your hair?" I told her it was going bye-bye and I asked her if she knew where it was going. She smiled and said, "Home." Here's a thought for all my fellow believers who are losing or have lost their hair. *What if God is collecting our lost hair in a jar to give it back to us in Heaven?*

Then, there will be no more hair plugs, ballcaps, nicked heads, or comb overs. TYJ

I want you to go to Heaven with me. If you are undernourished, like I was, I will be glad to help you on this journey. We do not need blueberries, sushi, bagels or nopales … we need our Daily Bread. I am going to leave you with something to chew on until the next chapter. **Read this carefully**: _**If you are not seated at the Lord's table eating the Bread of Life …You might find yourself on Satan's menu.**_

In the Lord's prayer, there is the phrase, *give us this day our daily bread.* Some people look at this from the physical sense and use it to mean He will provide enough food every day. There are others who refer to it as spending daily time in the Bible. Get Jesus and get nourished every day until you reach eternity. Here's a morsel of bread I ate today: *"**He chose to give us birth (life) through the word of truth, that we might be a kind of firstfruits of all He created."* James 1:18** I love this scripture because it connects the dots to Him who said I am the way, the truth, and the life. Dig for these scripture nuggets in the Word and it will *tune you into Wisdom.*

Salvation Station lesson #7 If you are not seated at the table eating from the Bread of God, you might find yourself on Satan's menu.

Recommended song to *tune you into the wisdom* about the message in this chapter is **Breath of Heaven** by Amy Grant. It can be found on YouTube and it includes the lyrics.

CHAPTER 8

THE LOVE OF CHRIST

Bear with each other and forgive one another if any of you has a grievance against someone. Forgive as the Lord forgave you. **Colossians 3:13**

*"**Unforgiveness** is the dam that restricts the love in your heart from flowing freely."* It creates a lake filled with anger, bitterness, and resentment. Don't allow your soul to be condemned by this poison. Forgive in the same manner Jesus did; **He forgave us to death**! Let the *Love of Christ* reign in your heart so the *Love of Christ* can rain from your heart.

Benita Orona (Gonzalez) An ordinary person touched by an Extraordinary God

She could have been bitter, felt self-pity, and been upset all her life because she was too young to remember her mother and never even saw a picture of her. Instead, she was content to hear that her mother was beautiful. Just being told about her mother was enough for Benita. All her life, she could have held onto *unforgiveness* towards her father as he gave her away and left never to be seen again when she was only 6 years old. In his defense, he did what he thought was best for his young daughter. This story is paraphrased from her daughter Brenda's tribute shown below. It is a remarkable story of how God intervened to help her grandfather find Benita in the late 1930s after her father had given her away to a couple that could not have children.

Think about this: It is 1939 and you live in Corpus Christi, Texas and your assignment is to find your granddaughter in Austin, Texas (population about 87,930 then). How do you start? Benita's grandfather did not even know the couple's name that Benita was given to. He had no address or clue of where to begin looking. He had to save up for bus fare to go from Corpus to Austin. There were no cell phones, maps at-a-glance, GPS, or Uber to help someone get around "big Austin." And even though WIFI had not been conceived yet, Grandpa had better – He had **SKY-FI** (prayer), a direct connection. **SKY-FI** has instant connection to God 24/7/365 without needing a 5G tower close by. So, boosted by prayer and blind faith, her grandfather set off on his journey of approximately 216 miles. His desire to find her was ignited with a blend of Heavenly fuel made from *the love of Christ*. What are the chances of finding her? Man's chances are slim and none, but with God anything is possible. *Do you agree with me that his finding Benita qualifies as an extraordinary miracle?*

She was born on March 23, 1933, and passed away on February 12, 2022.

Irma and I had the privilege of meeting Benita in 2002 when we were members of the newly formed Heart of Worship Christian Center. She was very quiet but commanded much attention just from her presence. She was a walking saint on earth. We kiddingly called her the 'movie star' because she was part of a church play. Even though she did not have a speaking part, Irma and I concluded she was the star of the show. Her stage presence exuded *the love of Christ*. When Benita did speak, she was like E.F. Hutton, so everyone listened, especially her children.

Her husband, Hector Gonzalez (RIP) was more flamboyant and full of wisdom. He was a Pastor for more than 50 years. I became close to him as I was hungry for the Word and he was always ready to share it "in season and out of season." He provided me with many words of wisdom. I wrote about him in Golden Walk in a chapter called, No Fear. My wish is Salvation Station will help readers have *no fear* of death, whatsoever. He told me three things that still resonate in my mind. *"We are not human beings having a spiritual experience, we are spiritual beings having a human experience."* He also told me, *"We only have this hour, so enjoy this moment."*

Lastly, he offered me, *"When you offer encouragement to others, it takes away your pain."*

In his last days, he demonstrated the above words of advice as he was receiving dialysis. I once went with him to understand the process. I watched many patients arriving by ambulance. Pastor Gonzalez walked in with cinnamon rolls to share and announced what a blessed man he was. It is my understanding he later passed away at that same the dialysis center. I was told when he walked in, the attendant asked him how he was. He responded, "I'm blessed, I'm blessed!" He then collapsed and was welcomed into Heaven by **Jesus**. Pastor Hector had *no fear* at his moment of death, and neither should we. Reverend Gonzalez spoke about his *love of Christ* until his last breath.

Benita and Hector had five children together, Hector Jr., Victor, Richard, Brenda, and Daniel. The sons later formed a group called Shekinah Glory that also included Jake Sanchez Sr. They sang Southern Gospel and in the height of their popularity were invited to appear on TBN. That show on TBN Praise The Lord was aired on April 28, 1992. You can look it up on YouTube and will be blessed to see Reverend Hector Gonzalez, Shekinah Glory and some guy named Jesse Duplantis. (smile)

The youngest brother named Daniel became my pastor and close friend. He passed away recently (October 11, 2022) and I had the privilege to read his obituary and share a few words of tribute at his Celebration of Life service in Midland, Texas. Prior to his passing into eternity, Dan had lost his eyesight and was blind. Even though he could not see, he always had vision. His vision came from the spiritual light in his heart and he also had a lamp to his feet. He knew where he was going as he saw his Reward waiting for him in Heaven. He suffered cardiac arrest and was without oxygen for 45 minutes. After he was rushed to the hospital, he remained unconscious on life support equipment. Knowing Pastor Dan like I did, I am confident that somewhere during his coma-like state, Dan's *desire* was for God to give him an opportunity to see Esther and his two sons Cailen and Kendall one last time. ***"When you delight in the Lord, He gives you the desires of your heart."* Psalm 37:4**

His wife Esther shared the following at the Celebration of Life Service. During his hospital stay, Dan did not wake up or talk. He was kept alive by medical equipment that provided oxygen and was nourished by IV (intravenous therapy). Removing life support is one of the hardest decisions a family has to make. After much prayer and 48 hours of deliberation, the medical equipment was unplugged. It was heart-wrenching to see the oxygen level go to zero as the heartbeat indicator went into a flat line. But, after a few seconds, they saw his heart start beating again. Dan opened his eyes and looked at each one of them intently. *The love of Christ* allowed Dan to see his wife and two sons one last time. When Esther realized he could see them, she told him, "It is okay to leave, we will be fine!" He closed his eyes and he was immediately in Heaven. Darkness cannot remain where the Light of Heaven shines! Thank you, Lord, for your goodness as this qualifies as *another one of your many miracles.*

Below is a copy of a Facebook posting that I asked Brenda Hobson for permission to place in Salvation Station. Brenda shares her love and admiration for her mother that had passed away one day prior to this posting on February 13, 2022. God bless you and Dale! The below is copied verbatim.

---

1 CORINTHIANS 13:4–8a
Love is patient and kind; love does not envy or boast; it is not arrogant or rude. It does not insist on its own way; it is not irritable or resentful; it does not rejoice at wrongdoing, but rejoices with the truth.

TODAY is a hard day! Yesterday @ 5:20 pm my mom Benita Gonzalez went home to be with the LORD. Mom was surrounded by family as she left from earth and entered heaven. Oh. how I miss her so much. I CELEBRATE Mom today and her precious life! This scripture so describes mom. I watched her live it and I saw it come to life in her life. My mom never met her mother. Even in her last days I was talking to her and said, "mom you are beautiful!" Her response was "thank you Brenda. That's what they would say about my mother.... I never did see her or even see a picture of her." Wow. She said it with no self pity or anger just love and being told that about her mother was ENOUGH. Her mother passed early in her life and her father gave her away to a couple who could not have children.

She had forgiven her father and she said I learned to pray. She couldn't remember who had taught her how to pray. Mom was in Austin Texas with this couple who loved her. Mom did not remember their names. One day they went to the stores in downtown Austin when my Grandfather who lived in Corpus went to find mom in Austin. He had no idea where she lived or how to find her. Her got off the bus determined that he would somehow find mom in big Austin. To his surprise he saw my mom in the back seat of a car and asked mom "Bena is that you?" It was! He waited for the couple to come back to their car. He explained who he was and that he had come from Corpus to find mom and he wanted to take mom back home to raise her with her family. So, Mom went with my grandfather. GOD began at moms early age to REVEAL HIS LOVE AND FAITHFULNESS. Mom decided in her early teens to give her life to the LORD and she NEVER LOOKED BACK.

She ran her race. She is now dancing in the presence of the LORD! 🙌🙏

THANK You Mom for loving me so unconditionally! THANK You Mom for being you and teaching me that GOD AND HIS WORD WAS ALL I NEEDED.

You forgave me everytime I fell. You helped to pick me up and encourage me. Although there were times you had to speak truth into me that at the time hurt…, you always did it in love and ended up by saying GOD WILL TURN THIS AROUND FOR GOOD in your life! (ROMANS 8:28)

I used to think I could NEVER LIVE ON WITHOUT You but today I KNOW I CAN AND I WILL! You GAVE ME THE WORD AND You GAVE me JESUS. JESUS, HIS WORD IN You were and are an example.

NO mistake, NO misfortune, NO unfairness, NO evil WILL EVER STOP GODS LOVE AND FAITHFULNESS in our lives. TODAY, I HOLD on TIGHTER to the WORD! I HOLD on TIGHTER TO THE

HOLY SPIRIT! I HOLD on TIGHTER TO my PRAYER LIFE! I HOLD on TIGHTER to ALL THAT You SAID TO me and TAUGHT me!

I AM FOREVER GRATEFUL!

HELP me HOLY SPIRIT TO DO THE SAME WITH MY CHILDREN.🙏🤝🖤

THANK YOU, FATHER, for my Precious Mom! Until we meet again,

I LOVE YOU FOREVER, your daughter, Brenda

Say Hi to JESUS! Say Hi to Dad, Hector and Vic! MISS THEM TOO!🖤🥹

The Homerun Disaster

Unforgiveness is not *the love of Christ* and builds a jail cell to be used for solitary confinement. It's made for the one that does not forgive. The bars for the cell are made from hard substances called anger, thoughts of revenge, hatred, and self-poison. It is difficult to escape and this confinement can lead to the *second death.* (more on this later in the book)

When I wrote my first book Barrio Walk: Stepping into Wisdom in 2019, I wrote about an unfair bullying experience that I was the victim of. After I had written the story, I realized I still had resentment for this bully more than 50 years later. You see, ***unforgiveness*** is a lonely place that sometimes gets buried so deep inside of you that only God can remove by shining His grace upon it. Sometimes the person, you are holding resentment for is completely unaware of your hurt or bitterness. *Take time to think about anyone you hold unforgiveness for. Use the <u>Lord's Prayer</u> as a guide, in part it says,* **"For if you forgive other people when they sin against you, your Heavenly Father will also forgive you." Matthew 6:14**

Do not allow the poison of unforgiveness to damn your soul to the separation from God forever.

The homerun disaster came toward the end of sixth grade at Jackson Elementary School in Phoenix, AZ. Back then, I was still innocent and a straight A student. I had also become a decent baseball player thanks to the excellent coaching from Armando Urias. We were undefeated and had a record of 13-0 during that year – it was a special time. I was physically in tip-top shape as I rode my bicycle to deliver the Arizona Republic in the morning before school and also after school to deliver the Phoenix Gazette.

There were two 6th grade classes at Jackson school and most kids went on to attend Grace Court for seventh and eighth grade prior to high school. The two sixth grade classes competed fiercely against each other in a variety of sports during our last recess in the afternoon. We competed in tug-of-war, track, dodge ball, football, and baseball. Many of us were good friends as we had already spent Kindergarten to 6th grade during those formative years.

During that 6th grade year, the other 6th grade class was increased by some new kids on the block that enrolled midway through the year. These kids seemed to be more street savvy and calloused as they came from the low-income housing near 15th Avenue and Buckeye. One of the kids was called The Kid and was 13 years old; most 6-graders are eleven years old. I stayed away from The Kid as he was a loud and boisterous bully. He could have passed for Clubber Lang's son from the movie Rocky II. He was harsh when he spoke and his words shot out of his mouth like nails. All the kids in the entire school were afraid of him.

Anyway, the homerun disaster happened near the end of one of our sixth-grade competitive baseball games. It was one of the most unfair things that happened to me in life at that point. I was a really good kid with straight A's. How many eleven-year olds have you ever known that could deliver newspapers before and after school seven days per week? During this baseball game, my class was trailing by a couple of runs, but we were batting in our final inning. It was the perfect scenario when it was my turn to bat.

There were two runners on base, and I was able to hit the ball perfectly. The ball sailed way over the left fielder's head almost to the swings. My classmates were cheering as I rounded the bases and getting ready to score the winning run. I went from *glory to unglory* with a swing of the bat and a trot around the bases. The Kid was upset and stood in the way so I could not cross home plate. There were no coaches or teachers monitoring our game. I tried to tell him we won fair and square. He was ticked off at me and told me to shut up. Since there was no adult presence, he began punching me and gave me a good beating. It was shocking and unfair to go from a hero to getting pummeled by a bully and losing all dignity in a blink of an eye.

I wish I could see The Kid today so I could challenge him to a rematch now. (**Note to reader: When I wrote this more than 50 years later, I realized I still had unforgiveness for The Kid. It made me pause in writing and forgive the Kid.**) The beating hurt me physically but I felt more upset because none of my friends intervened. Over the years I had defended several of them before at various times. There was no one who stepped in or tried to stop The Kid.

I was too embarrassed to go back into the classroom after recess so I went home without telling anyone in authority. This was a major violation of a Jackson School rule that had been engrained into me for the past seven years at that point.

I went home limping and sobbing with my pants torn. I had blood on my knee and my head throbbed with every step I took. My nose had a trickle of blood that I smeared onto my forearm. I also felt a "small mouse" forming under my left eye. When I got home, my Tia Tillie (RIP) was visiting my mom. They were both surprised to see me crying and home from school about an hour ahead of schedule. My aunt was livid when I told them what had happened; she used some strong and colorful language I did not expect from her. My mother just said, "You better toughen up, boy!"

My aunt went on to say, "We are getting in my car right now so we can go find him RIGHT NOW. I'm going to hold him down and you are going to pound him!" I was worried and told my aunt he was pretty tough. She looked at me with a scowl that would have made Jack Nicholson jealous and said very emphatically "HE DOES NOT KNOW WHAT TOUGH IS!!!" Next thing I knew we were in her car and on a mission to seek and destroy. We went looking for him on what I thought would be his route home to his roach-infested, ghetto tenement (*I was upset when I wrote this the first time*). We did not find him that day and it was probably better for two reasons:

1. My Tia Tillie could not be with me every day for the remainder of sixth grade.
2. It was 1964 and I did not learn the crane kick from The Karate Kid movie until 1984 (LOL).

After the homerun disaster, I feared meeting up with The Kid while I was on my paper route after school. My worry was he would take away any money my customers had paid me for paper delivery. My confidence was shaken, and I used to practice making mean faces in front of the mirror. I used to curse The Kid and his mother with vulgar language in my dark moments when unforgiveness overwhelmed me.

After a few weeks, The Kid met up with me once while I was on my paper route. He managed to straddle the front tire of my bicycle and grab the handlebars. He grinned at me and sneered, "Hello Ruben." He had two sets of sutures (stitches) over one of his eyebrows and on the bridge of his nose. The cuts were fresh and I could see a hint of iodine on them. Even though it was daytime, the scene could have been called *Fright Night*. It was sheer terror for me, but adrenaline kicked in and I was able to get loose from his grasp and ride away without words or confrontation. I'm so thankful God was in control.

Perhaps, God gave me an advance on protection even though at the time, I did not have a personal relationship with Him yet. After all, it does say in the Book of **Proverbs 16:7,** *"When the Lord takes pleasure in anyone's way, He causes their enemies to be at peace with them."* My comfort now comes from knowing this promise, *"**The Lord himself goes before you and will be with you; he will never leave you nor forsake you. Do not be afraid; do not be discouraged"** (**Deuteronomy 31:8**).

Post note: The night after I wrote this chapter, I reread it and the realization came to me that I still had bitterness over this incident more than 55 years ago. I also remembered wishing bad things would happen to The Kid and his family. I prayed and asked God to shine His light into my heart and remove my unforgiveness toward The Kid. God was good enough to take that poison out of me.

God took care of it, and in this forgiving process, it removed this little defect and took away some of that darkness that had long been embedded in my heart. The remarkable thing about forgiving someone even though it might be the last thing you want to do—it sets the prisoner free. The prisoner is not the person who did you wrong, the prisoner is really you. Sometimes the offender has no clue you are holding a grudge. The poison from the unforgiveness hardens your heart and takes away life flow with thoughts of revenge or other forms of wishing evil on your offender.

Whoever that person is, make time to forgive them and move on with life more freely. It is good for your heart, almost like eating Applejacks, you know the slogan if you are old enough: "*A bowl a day, keeps the bullies away*!" That's what I used to think, but now I know that if I keep my heart full of the *love of Christ* and wear the Armor of God daily, my remaining days on the 'third rock from the sun' are bully-proof.

Joseph the Dreamer

If there is one person in the Bible that was the most likely succeed in being filled with unforgiveness it is Joseph. He was born to Jacob whose name was changed to Israel. His story is one of my favorites and can be found in the Book of Genesis in Chapters 37 to 50. Joseph was one of twelve brothers from the tribe of Israel. I strongly encourage you to read it.

It speaks of the many hardships Joseph suffered in life. He was his father Jacob's favorite son and when Jacob gave Joseph a coat of many colors, his brothers looked at him with pickle-colored eyes filled with jealousy. These ill feelings became more harsh after Joseph told his brother of two dreams involving them. In both dreams, he was portrayed as ruling over his family. In the first, the brothers were gathering wheat in the field, and the brothers' bundles of wheat bowed to Joseph's bundle. In the second, Joseph envisioned the sun, the moon, and eleven stars (symbolizing his parents and brothers) were all bowing to him.

They made fun of Joseph and called him 'dreamer'. One day, Jacob instructed Joseph to visit his brothers in Shechem, where they were tending their sheep. Little did Jacob know that this would be the last time he would see his dear Joseph until their reunion a long twenty-two years later.

The brothers decided to get rid of Joseph once and for all so they threw their unsuspecting younger brother into a pit. A short while later they spotted an Arab caravan passing by their location and the brothers sold Joseph to the traders. He was eventually brought to Egypt, where he was sold to Potiphar, one of King Pharaoh's ministers. The brothers applied animal blood to his coat of many colors and told their father that Joseph had been killed by wild animals.

Joseph was taken to Egypt and sold to the captain of the guard, Potiphar, as a household slave. Later, he was accused of attempting to rape Potiphar's wife. She had attempted to seduce Joseph and mendaciously accused him of wrongdoing after he rejected her. As a result, he was thrown into prison. Joseph had a gift that allowed him to interpret dreams. This gift of discernment got him out of jail. Subsequently, he was able to interpret the Pharaoh's dream in such a powerful way that Joseph was appointed as second in command over Egypt. There are many more details in this story that I am confident will *tune you into wisdom*. You will get so much more from reading Joseph's entire story directly from the Bible. Connect with **SKY-FI** prior to reading this worthwhile story.

A Lesson in Forgiveness

Joseph's story highlights the proper attitude toward difficulty and misfortune. He remained faithful to God and was rewarded. Because there was a severe famine in Egypt, his brothers arrived to buy food. After discovering Joseph's identity, his brothers were sure he would utilize his imperial powers to get revenge against them for their evil conduct. The brothers came to Joseph to beg for forgiveness. Joseph wept when he heard their appeal. Revenge was the last thing on his mind. What Joseph expressed to them was quite the opposite: *"Don't be afraid. Am I in place of God? You intended to harm me, but God intended it for good to accomplish what is now being done, the saving of many lives. So then, don't be afraid. I will provide for you and your children."* **Genesis 50: 20-21**.

Joseph recognized that all the pitfalls, pardon the pun, he had undergone were ordained by God to ensure the survival of Egypt and the surrounding countries. Keeping this in mind enabled him to forgive his brothers and repay animosity with benevolence. Joseph's words to his brothers in their moment of fear was full of the love of Christ.

This story has many lessons on various subjects such as, fatherly love, sibling rivalry, jealousy, unwavering faith, and most importantly *forgiveness*. This is an excellent point to pause in the reading of this book and spend time in Joseph's story found in the book of Genesis beginning in Chapter 37. No matter where you are in life, stay faithful to God, and He will help you in your journey of life. Joseph was just an ordinary person, like us, touched by an extraordinary God.

Salvation Station lesson # 8: Let the Love of Christ, His perfect love, allows you to be you and me to be me.

Recommended song to *tune you into the wisdom* about the message in this chapter is **Greatest Love of All**, by Whitney Houston. You can find it with lyrics on YouTube.

CHAPTER 9

WE ALL HAVE SCARS

"Look at my Hands and my Feet. It is I myself. Touch me and see; a ghost does not have flesh and bone, as you see I have." **Luke 24:39**

After Jesus had been crucified and laid in a tomb, the 11 remaining disciples scattered and were afraid like a flock without a shepherd while the wolves are nearby – their Hope was gone. On that third morning, they found that empty tomb filled with signs (his bloodstains and burial cloths and linens) that He had risen. At the tomb Peter 'saw the strips of linen by themselves, and he went away, wondering to himself what had happened.' (Luke 24:12b)

Later that day on the road to Emmaus, Jesus walked with two of his followers, one of them was named Cleopas. They talked about all that had happened during His crucifixion and the finding of the empty tomb. These disciples did not recognize Jesus until He took bread, gave thanks, and began to give it to them. Then, their eyes were open and they recognized Him and He disappeared from their sight. (Do your research and find this story in the book of Luke, chapter 24)

These two disciples at once returned to Jerusalem to tell the others what had happened and how they recognized Him after He broke the bread. As they were telling the story of seeing Jesus on the road to Emmaus, He appeared before the disciples, they were terrified and thought they were looking at a ghost. He told them, look at my scars, l am not a ghost. They had a hard time believing Jesus had risen as they were filled with joy and amazement.

He asked them if they had anything to eat and they gave him a piece of broiled fish. He was Alive and he showed them His scars to prove it. He left us with instructions to take communion in remembrance of Him.

Irma and I had a beautiful breakfast this morning as we discussed the Road to Emmaus in detail and how He ate with His disciples and showed them His scars to prove He was not a ghost. We nourished our day by taking two small pieces of tortilla, breaking them, and giving thanks in memory of what He did for us. We also finished by drinking juice to represent the Blood He shed for the remission of our sins. Some people may think we are not credentialed enough to share the Lord's Supper at home. I object! I strongly object – this is why. It is about obedience and He told us to do it.

We received a command from our Lord to share bread and wine to commemorate His death. I always look forward to partaking in this ceremonial meal as it connects me more closely to Jesus. This act of obedience makes us remember Your last supper, Your broken body, and Your sin-cleansing blood. The Lord's Supper is about You solely, it focuses us on the reason You came to earth. It is no longer about the Law or Abraham, Isaac, and Jacob. It is remembering You are the Lamb of God— the Only One who takes away the sin of the world.

Communion is a sacred form of worship that we should prepare ourselves spiritually before receiving it. Whether you take this special meal in the privacy of your home or at your local church, we must never take this privilege for granted or lightheartedly. Here is a short prayer as a suggestion to help prepare you for receiving the Lord's supper.

Lord Jesus, I humbly come before You and ask You to examine my heart right now. Reveal to me anything that is not pleasing to You. Show me any secret pride, any unconfessed sin, or unforgiveness that may be hindering my relationship with You. Thank You for Your extravagant love and sacrifice. I'm grateful because Your death gave me life—abundant life for now, and eternal life for eternity. I pray this with admiration in Your precious Name. Amen.

The Lord took those scars to Heaven, *will you be worthy of seeing them?*

Ruben Gonzales

We All Have Scars

All of us have scars – some are still healing. We have to practice empathy rather than pulling someone's scab off. *Empathy is the ability to understand and share the feelings of another.* We cannot judge why someone is behaving like they do until we find out what caused this behavior.

For example, I heard a story of a man and a young boy who had just gotten on the Metro in Washington DC. The man seemed despondent while the young boy was causing a ruckus with all his ranting and raving. A woman quickly told the man, "Calm down your son and make him behave normal!" The man responded, "His behavior might be normal for a 6-year old who just saw his mother die from cancer."

What scars do you have? Are they wounds from a war? Are they memories from a war? Is it the unseen constant ringing in your ears? How about the harsh words of rejection? Sticks and stones may break my bones, but words can break my heart. How many times have you judged someone who does not look handicapped but uses that parking privilege? Their handicap might be internal or not readily seen through eyes without empathy.

My worst physical scar comes from a knee operation I incurred while playing football that resulted in a torn meniscus way back in 1975. The scar does not hurt any more, but the pain increases when the outside temperature decreases. I'm grateful to still have the same knee I was born with and the ability to exercise almost daily. It's been fun telling my little buddy (grandson who shares my birthday), that my scar came from a war wound while on my ship in Vietnam.

This farfetched grandpa story ends with my cut had to be stitched by a medic using fishing line and a fishhook while the ship was rocking violently. Of course, I turned it into a lesson of forgiveness and knew it was effective about a week after our talk. Iven asked me, "Grandpa are you still mad at the guy who shot you in the knee? I had to tell him the truth and he told me, "That's okay – I love hearing your stories."

Whatever your scar came from, Jesus experienced them all and then some. Some were the ones you can't see, those emotional ones when you receive bad news. How would you feel if your first cousin (Jesus' cousin was John the Baptist) got his head cut off and his head placed on a platter at Herod's birthday celebration? (read about this in Matthew chapter 14) With one thought Jesus could have beheaded King Herod and all those attending his party. Jesus could have sent multiple platters of severed heads directly into the Lake of Fire with one thought of revenge. He was without sin and became eternally scarred because of our sins.

Jesus was disfigured and unrecognizable by the time He was nailed to the cross. He received punches, slaps, a crown of thorns, stripes on his back from being scourged with a whip, scrapes from falling underneath the weight of the cross and then those nails that went through His Hands and Feet. These are the only scars we'll see in Heaven. What if Jesus would have said, "Abba Father, I can't take this, let's go to plan B." Plan B being the destruction of humanity at that moment. Instead, He felt the agony of abandonment when He cried out, "My God, My God why have thou forsaken me." He did not deserve this, but He did it because He had each one of us on His mind.

He experienced death and survived it. He was not scared and we should have no fear of death either. Because of Him, now when we die, we have The Only One who can show us how to escape from the grave and live with Him. He also said He has gone to prepare a place for us. Just think, He owns the universe and can build our residence from material unknown by us. What an incredible Savior we have, scarred by our sins and still loving us enough to prepare a place we do not deserve.

"Cast your cares on the Lord and He will sustain you ..." Psalm 55:22

"Only Good Days and Better Days!"

That is the life motto my friend Rick Garza has made as his mantra after suffering a major setback more than fifty years ago. He is the prime example of knowing to trust in God. This comes by (in his words) understanding to accept the things we can't change and to let go of what we can't control. It took courage for him to share his scars as he relived the day, and aftermath, that changed his life forever.

He woke up while it was still dark outside to the lingering smell of coffee throughout the house. His mom got up extra early to make biscuits, bacon & eggs, and the best salsa in Laredo, Texas. His parents and his sister Rosie were filled with excitement as they loaded up the car. His father's 1967 Caprice was impeccable and looked like it had just come out of the dealership showroom. Rick had dreams of driving this beauty to high school. It was painted metallic gold and sported a white vinyl top. The 327 cubic inch engine hummed perfectly and riding in it was pure, exquisite comfort.

Life could not have been sweeter, there he was, a 13-year old son, just enjoying the ride with his father, mother and sister headed from Laredo to Fort Worth. Like most typical Mexican-American families, they joked about getting past the 11-mile marker known as the Border Patrol Checkpoint. They were on their way to relish a family day with his older brother who was serving in the Air Force. Rick loved riding shotgun while studying the map so he could verbally navigate the directions to his father. However, that morning his mother had asked him if she could ride in the front seat as her arthritis in her knee was flaring up. A prompting from Above seemed to have given her a premonition that the front seat was her destiny, not her son's.

That early Friday morning before the sunrise seemed so perfect as he was talking man-to-man with his dad without a care in the world. They talked about life and Rick's musical dreams as he had learned to play the trumpet. He had been inspired by his father's love of hearing music by Herb Alpert and the Tijuana Brass on his 8-track player. Rick was a non-stop chatterbox that continued to tell his father about his love for golf and sports. Abruptly, a thought bubble popped into his brain as he looked at his sweet mom who was enjoying the trip – relaxing with her contented eyes closed. He thought, I could enjoy the sights much better if I was in the front seat. He quickly got rid of this selfish thought as his heart smiled at his mom; she was the love of his young life. His sister was with him in the backseat sleeping comfortably. They shared a Styrofoam ice chest as an armrest between them.

Suddenly, his dad shouts out to him, "Aguila!" as his father moved quickly to his right to hold his wife's chest with his arm . . . those were Rick's *last thoughts* of his mom & dad. His dad's *last words* (Aguila is Spanish slang that means stay alert; keep your head on a swivel) only to be followed by complete silence. He looked up to see the *last glimpse* of reality that was a rather large object heading into their lane on that dreadful morning. The eerie sound of stillness, darkness, and quietness also collided shortly after the 18-wheeler hit them head-on. His father had tried desperately to avoid the collision with the massive truck as they were going around a curve; only to have his beautiful prized-possession smeared against the guard rail. His father's side of the car took the brunt of the impact while his mother was trapped in a tangled mess. There were no jaws of life back then to save her. He lost his parents in an instant leaving him with lifelong scars engraved into his soul.

It wasn't too long before Rick heard the sound of the shifting of gears coming from the back of the wreckage and his semi-consciousness. He does not remember this but later found out a good Samaritan kicked down the back windshield and wrestled death to pull him and his 16-year old sister out of the back seat. This unknown person rushed them to the closest ER in Pearsall, Texas and left them there. This hero provided sketchy information, and to this day, they do not know the name of this angel God dispatched to save them.

Rick awakened to the screams of his sister in the Pearsall emergency room as he struggled to locate her. They told him to remain still as the medical team was finishing the last of forty seven stitches on his head. This is when he first felt the pain in his ribs and his right hand throbbed as he almost lost his pointer finger. His face, head and hands were covered with blood and he was surprised to see his favorite psychedelic shirt had been cut in half and on the floor. It looked different because it had some additional red stains on it. Rick also suffered a cracked skull, a concussion, a broken rib cage, a hyperextended knee and multiple lacerations to his face and hand.

He continued to hear his sister screaming as she had just been forcefully awakened from unconsciousness. She had a severe laceration to her cheek, a broken jaw and was in the state of shock. He was told to relax while they repaired his sister and he would see her soon in a private room. Rick was wheeled to a room where he joined his sister. She began to cry and he reassured her they were going to be okay. He was able to tell her they had been involved in a head-on collision prior to his oldest sister arriving in their room.

Rick's sister and brother fought back tears when told by Pearsall hospital personnel not to mention that their parents had been killed in the accident. His first questions to his siblings was, "Where are mom and dad?' They replied, "They're in a hospital in San Antonio and are doing well." His sister went on to say, "Mom said for you to eat." She knew Rick was a finicky eater. At home he only ate tortillas, beans, bacon, egg yolk and hamburger steak - nothing else! So, each subsequent day his siblings visited him, they kept stressing how mom said he'd better eat the food they gave him. He mostly ate toast and jello. His sister Rosie could only eat pureed food for the next 6-8 weeks because her jaw was wired shut. Several days later, Rick and his sister were transferred to Mercy Hospital in Laredo.

He vividly remembers the trip in an ambulance heading south on Interstate 35. They were greeted by a welcoming party of aunts, uncles, cousins, and Grandma Gila, who they called Mama Abuelita. The family thought it was best not to tell him about his parents and how he had already missed their funerals during his recovery in the hospital. Who knows if it was right to keep him from the closure that comes from a burial? Perhaps the horrible news would have been too much for this 13-year old and would have caused him to give up on life.

During their visits, Rick kept asking his siblings, "When are mom and dad coming to Laredo?" Their answer was always 'they should be here in a week or so.' Something was not adding up in Rick's mind because he should have at least talked to his parents by phone by now. During his lengthy stay, he sometimes wondered if he would ever leave this Hospital of Mercy that he had been born in thirteen years prior.

When Rick was born the doctor who delivered him nicknamed him 'the wheelchair baby'. This was because his head was popping outside of his mother's womb when they brought her in on a wheelchair. His arrival into the world included being transported into Mercy hospital in a wheelchair. His life came full circle as he was about to leave that same hospital to face a changed world.

The day he had so waited for was finally here. Rick's overall condition was finally stable enough to go home. He felt badly saying goodbye to his sister who was still fragile as she was still recovering from mental shock. He looked with sadness at his sister from a wheelchair but knew it was best for her to stay while she recovered.

As he was being wheeled out toward the hall floor, he was surprised to see the doctor who had nicknamed him the wheelchair baby. This doctor took over in wheeling him towards the elevator. He gave instructions to other people waiting for the elevator to wait for the next one to arrive. As Rick and the doctor entered the elevator alone and the doors closed, the doctor asked him, "Do you know where your mom and dad are?" He quickly replied, "Yes, in San Antonio!" He seriously looked at him and said, "NO SON, THEY'RE DEAD!" Those words blasted into Rick's head like an atomic bomb. Those insensitive words seemed to rip the outer layer that encased his heart (the pericardium). The doctor was completely out of line to give Rick this horrific news. It was as if the doctor pulled off a scab before it even began to heal. "*The tongue has the power of life and death*" **Proverbs 18:21** (*Note: this is equivalent to someone posting of someone's death on Facebook before the immediate next of kin even know about it*)

Rick felt instant numbness as the anticipation and hope of seeing his parents departed from his soul. He did not know how to react – Was this a sick joke? Should he be angry? It seemed like an unbelievable nightmare but he was fully awake. It was a *full circle*. . . the doctor who brought him into the world when he entered the hospital in a wheelchair, now delivered him into a world of harsh reality and brutal truth as Rick was leaving that same hospital in a wheelchair.

Rick told me after reflecting on that moment, he vowed to treasure every moment of every day and have "No bad days in life!" and spend "Only Good Days and Better Days!"

His wheelchair ride to his sister's car was long and silent. He couldn't help but notice his siblings expressionless, somber faces. He saw his own lost empty expression in the refection of his sister's eyes. His sister Anna took the role as his second mom and she did a fabulous job of keeping the family intact. The loss of their parents solidified their family like a rock.

Rick spent the next couple of days resting at home. He soon experienced the looks from his classmates that wanted to look at the stitch marks on his head without being noticed. *They did not know what to say.* He remembers the embarrassment of trying to walk in front of his buddies only to take a hard fall on the patio floor. The absence of mom and dad was immense as he struggled through life. During the holidays, he knew the celebrations would never be the same. Sometimes it seemed like bittersweet tears were flowing down from Heaven. Perhaps that is why he always looks up at the rain and smiles. His parents were not there to see his children born, or to help him with his subsequent divorce after being married for 20 years.

Rick is forever believing in God - His Love prevails in Rick's life to this day. He has learned some valuable lessons to get over his grief. A person can get stuck in grief if they continue to only listen to that song of pity over and over again. Life must go on and you have to make the most of it. One of the things I learned from spending time with Rick during this writing process is that grief never ends but it changes. *It is a passage, not a place you want to get stuck in. Grief is not a sign of weakness or lack of Faith . . . It is the Price of Love.*

Rick Garza leaves you with three of the Lord's powerful lessons he received:

1. Never to take things for granted
2. Stop and smell those roses.
3. Tomorrow is not promised.

Today, if you ask Rick how he is, he will wholeheartedly respond with, "It's another day in Paradise!" He continues to preach how wonderful life is at work and lives life to the fullest.

His co-workers and other people he meets have said, "Are you high or something? You are always so happy." I met him in 2018 during my last days in an official work capacity. He is one of the most loyal friends I have known in my life. You'll love him if you meet him as he celebrates life as he cherishes each moment. He loves to take selfies with you without warning. Be ready to eat because he loves to cook and is generous with sharing his salsa and his specialty of lemon tilapia.

It touched me when he agreed to joined me in golfing. It was something he was no longer interested in since those long ago days on the golf course with his father.

Golfing again!

He honored me with his friendship and trusted me to tell his story written for the Glory of God alone. I'm proud of him having the courage to show us his scars and how he overcame them. He told me how he had to relive moments he has repressed all his life. He said somehow, even though it was difficult, it was also therapeutic. Today, he resides with his wife Beth of eight years, who, in his words, "Is way more than he deserves." As Rick likes to say, "He continues in Surviving 13 in Good and Better Days!"

Sometimes scars are not seen and they cause grooves that mar someone's soul. If a person gets stuck there, it can impede their love from flowing and keeps them stuck in the past. Rick could have given up on life but instead he learned to trust and thank God every day for every breath and every moment. Soli Deo Gloria!

We all have scars but we won't take them with us to Heaven.

Salvation Station Lesson # 9 Life is precious and it can be taken from us at any moment.

Recommended song to *tune you into the wisdom* about the message in this chapter is: ***Scars in Heaven*** by Casting Crowns. You can find it with lyrics on YouTube.

CHAPTER 10

SURVIVOR

Once we fully grasp that we are spiritual beings living in a temporary human body, it gives us the freedom to <u>survive</u> anything in this life.

Our whole world can be changed in an instant with one phone call. Our Faith can be tested with one medical report. Who's report will you believe? The human one that says there is no hope or are you going to believe in the Promise that tells us *by Whose stripes you **were healed***. The one report is made from temporary human words; the Other is the Truth – the eternal Word of God.

Please *tune into wisdom* as you read this extraordinary story from Shelly Smith Morales. It is in her words verbatim.

Shelly's Story of Faith in Action

The crisp mountain air revved my lungs as I strode out of the Colorado Springs airport with my luggage and headed through the parking lot to pick up my rental car. The conference for Aglow International I was co-leading that weekend was something I'd been looking forward to since the year before and now it was almost here.

I eased the rental car onto the highway and towards the road that would take me to my hotel. My mind buzzed with conference details, the majesty of my surroundings, and anticipation with what God would do in us that weekend.

My phone rang. I didn't recognize the number but answered anyway. My surgeon's clear voice greeted me.

She'd done a biopsy on me a few days before but had assured me she didn't feel there was anything to worry with.

Now, though, her voice was tinged with concern. "Shelly, I hope you're not alone."

I told her I was and that I was in Colorado Springs, a long way from our home in South Texas.

She cleared her throat. "I wish there was a better way to tell you this. I'm so sorry, but the results of breast biopsy we did on you shows cancer and we believe it is advanced and aggressive."

I thought perhaps I had fallen asleep at the wheel and was dreaming.

"Shelly, are you there?" she asked carefully.

I mumbled something in reply, realizing I wasn't dreaming. "You need to come home now as we have appointments set up for you already, " she told me firmly.

I couldn't breathe.

I assured her I would find a return flight home. I pulled over and called my husband, Joe. As stunned as he was, he prayed a powerful prayer. I quickly called and made arrangements for the conference as I navigated back to the airport, I'd just left not 30 minutes earlier.

I located a flight that would get me home, but not until the early morning.

I found my way to a small waiting area near the terminal I would be departing from, and sitting on a small bench, surrounded by my luggage, I put my head in my hands.

Finally, I squeezed out a simple phrase of prayer. "Lord, what next?"

A gentle Voice came forth in my spirit.

"Shelly, establish now in your heart how you will show up in this."

Although I knew that was the Holy Spirit, I'd expected something more comforting and reassuring. I asked out loud, "What?"

Again, I heard and knew He was speaking in my spirit. "Establish now how you will show up in this."

I came up with several things, like:

I will respond with faith in You, Lord, not fear.

I will be strong and courageous.

I will give thanks in all things.

I will believe Your Word over anything else.

He was wounded for our transgressions, He was bruised for our iniquities. The chastisement of our peace was upon Him, and by His stripes, we are healed. Isaiah 53:5

The next weeks were a blur of many tests, meetings with the oncologist and surgeon, and having a mediport surgically installed in my chest to receive chemo.

I devoured His Word, starting in the gospels of the New Testament, when Jesus walked the earth and performed signs, wonders, and miracles. The more I read and reread of Jesus' walk on this earth, (although I'd known Him as my Lord and Savior for many decades), the more my faith grew.

After all the tests, the oncologist reported that the cancer was stage 4, the worst. I would be treated with aggressive chemo, immunotherapy (just approved by the FDA for this type of cancer only months before), then surgery, and the final piece would be radiation. I could see the looks on the faces of medical professionals as they read my records. They weren't looks of hope, and they offered none with their words.

Joe and I prayed continually and he daily bolstered my faith with his calm, steady, and unshakeable belief in God's Word.

At my next oncologist's appointment, I asked the Lord for hope from a doctor. The oncologist acknowledged that it was quite serious, and usually stage 4 means no cure. He said, "But with you, Shelly, I'm going for a cure, not just a management plan of cancer."

That one voice of hope gave me more strength. Finally, an earthly voice in the medical community agreed with God's Word.

I decided then I wouldn't accept anything that didn't agree with God's Word. Humans can be educated and deal in facts, but God, from Whom all wisdom flows, deals in truth.

Dear friends and family prayed for me in agreement with God's Word:

Who Himself bore our sins in His own body on the tree, that we, having died to sins might live for righteousness, by Whose stripes you were healed. 1 Peter 2:24

They warred with us, remembering that *we do not wrestle against flesh and blood, but against principalities, against powers, against rulers of darkness of this age, against spiritual hosts of wickedness in heavenly places. Ephesians 6:12*

I searched for and read testimonies of healing from cancer by various people. I read Kathryn Kuhlman's books filled with testimonies of healing and on her reliance on the Holy Spirit. I read and studied F.F. Bosworth's book, Christ the Healer. I found Dodie Osteen's book, Healed of Cancer, and read through many times her testimony of being healed by God of stage 4 cancer and being given only a few weeks to live. She included a list of 40 healing scriptures in her book.

I read the Word out loud and declared those 40 healing scriptures aloud daily. I also prayed through each of them as I declared them.

It was clear to me that it is just as much God's will for us to be healed as it is His will for us to be saved.

My mind asked why this was happening. "Why" is a faith negating question and I couldn't pursue it and build my faith at the same time. I closed off that door in my thinking. *Now faith is the substance of things hoped for, the evidence of things not seen. For by it the elders obtained a good testimony. By faith we understand that the ʿworlds were framed by the word of God, so that the things which are seen were not made of things which are visible. Hebrews 11:1-3*

The chemo caused my hair to fall out and for deep fatigue to hit me periodically. But skipping my times with the Lord each day was never an option.

I loved being with Him.

I enjoyed His Presence.

His Word was a delight to me. Though my voice sometimes sounded like a croak, I read it aloud in His Presence.

Soon, I felt the Holy Spirit telling me to limit what I read to Godly books, like Ruben Gonzales' books Barrio Walk, Broken Walk, and Golden Walk. I quit looking up things about cancer on Google after I felt the Holy Spirit chasten me one day. "Who do you believe- Google, or me?"

Taking communion daily brought great joy to us. *And when He had taken a cup and given thanks, He said, "Take this and share it among yourselves; for I say to you, I will not drink of the fruit of the vine from now on until the kingdom of God comes." And when He had taken some bread and given thanks, He broke it and gave it to them, saying, "This is My body, which is being given for you; do this in remembrance of Me." And in the same way He took the cup after they had eaten, saying, "This cup, which is poured out for you, is the new covenant in My blood. Luke 22: 17-20*

I went through my heart to unload any unforgiveness or bitterness I might be holding. Faith doesn't operate in an environment contaminated with that. *So, as those who have been chosen of God, holy and beloved, put on a heart of compassion, kindness, humility, gentleness, and patience; bearing with one another, and forgiving each other, whoever has a complaint against anyone; just as the Lord forgave you, so must you do also. Colossians 3:12-13*

Finally, after six months of chemo, it was time for the surgery. The surgeon sent everything he removed to pathology. After a time of recuperation, we met with the surgeon and the oncologist.

The surgeon said it was quite remarkable and couldn't keep the wide grin from his face. The oncologist called it phenomenal and said, "By the grace of God, you are cancer free! It's all gone!"

The written pathology report and the other tests gave testimony to what God had done. From stage 4 cancer to stage 0- meaning no cancer in my body. I don't have cancer anywhere. And by the oncologist's own words, it is by God's grace, mercy, power, might, and compassion.

There are a few who say a person is never truly healed of cancer, that it can come back. It won't in me. I reply with the Word of God: *"...Affliction will not rise up a second time." Nahum 1:9*

God is no respecter of persons. He healed me and He will heal you. It may not come overnight, as happened in my case, but His Word is true, and our part is to believe Him all the way through.

Dear friend, I pray that you may enjoy good health and that all may go well with you, even as your soul is getting along well. 3 John 2

Below is a copy of the email I received from Shelly sent to me on January 20, 2023 at 6:06 AM.

Had an appointment with the oncologist yesterday. He had a huge smile. He read through the pathology reports and recent lab work and said by the grace of God, I am now cancer free! Hallelujah!!! I will still go through radiation as it helps keep it from recurring. He said it is phenomenal, this response to what had been identified back in June as Stage 4 cancer. How faithful our Lord is!!! His Word never fails!!!

Thank you both so much for your continuing prayers. We love you and Irma – so appreciate you two for your Holy Spirit led prayers and encouragement.

At this point, I want to take time to brag on Shelly because she prefers to stay humble. Just this morning, I was blessed to see her message on Facebook. I can hardly wait to read her first book. Her message today blessed me and many others. This is an example of who she is and what she does. She is an incredible Woman of God and gifted photographer. Here is her posting:

Christ with me,
Christ before me,
Christ behind me,
Christ in me,
Christ beneath me,
Christ above me,
Christ on my right,
Christ on my left,
Christ when I lie down,
Christ when I sit down,
Christ when I arise,
Christ in the heart of every man who thinks of me,
Christ in the mouth of everyone who speaks of me,
Christ in every eye that sees me,
Christ in every ear that hears me.

When Shelly learned of her devastating report, she turned up the volume on her gratitude. She began listing daily five things she was grateful for.

She also encouraged others to do the same. At last check, there are 217 days of postings from her Facebook friends giving God daily thanks. This has caused thousands of messages based on gratitude. *(One of mine included, "I love the smell of rain in the desert during a summer morning. It is as if the ground is sending up a scent of gratitude.)* This 'gratitude chain' came without asking for prayer for herself. Most are still presently unaware of her temporary setback brought on by that C word that no longer exists in her.

God loves it when we give thanks and it is even more special to Him when we give *thanks in advance* based on Faith. Take a hard look at what it says about Faith in action in **Hebrews 11:1** *Now faith is confidence in what we hope for and assurance about what we do not see.*

Last summer, Irma and I were on our way to Arizona. We called Shelly and we were surprised because she it did not sound like herself as her voice was deeper and sounded raspy. She went on to tell us she had been diagnosed with Stage 4 cancer and was receiving treatment. She told us she was just beginning a process to eradicate this aggressive form of cancer. We were stunned by this news and immediately began praying with her. Part of the prayer included giving God thanks in advance for Shelly's complete healing. I told her that I would hold a reserved place in this book so she could write about her experience about the complete healing she received. So, **there it is** – the word of Shelly's testimony to increase our Faith and bring Glory to God. Glory to the King of all kings, the Lord of lords!!! He is worthy!!! His Faithfulness continues to all generations!!! Worthy is the Lamb of God who takes away the sin of the world!!!

Thank You, Jesus because by Your stripes *we were healed.* Thank you, Shelly for sharing your story so others can know if it happened for you it can happen for them. God bless you and Joe, your daughters, and your precious mom.

Gratitude - One Came Back to Say Thanks

The book of Luke, Chapter 17: 11-19 tells of Jesus encountering ten men who were lepers that lifted up their voices asking for mercy. *"So, when He saw them, He said to them, "Go, show yourselves to the priests." And so it was that as they went, they were cleansed."* Back in those days, people with leprosy were required by law to keep away from healthy people (Leviticus 13:46); these ten lepers came as close as they dared and called out loudly to Jesus. Please notice the words as they went. Perhaps their healing had to do with obedience and <u>as they went</u>, they were cleansed. They received their physical cleansing from leprosy by acting in obedience to Jesus command when he told them to go show themselves to the priest. Obedience and following His Instructions activated the miracle to restore their flesh, perhaps there was more for them from Jesus if those nine lepers had gone back to give thanks.

Naaman had to dip himself in the water of the Jordan River seven times before his flesh was restored from leprosy like the flesh of a little child. (2 Kings: 5:14). The Israelites had to march around the Walls of Jericho seven times before the walls came crashing down. What miracle do you need? Sometimes it may take faith combined with obedience to make it happen . . . all in God's timing.

So, to take it a step further, when you receive your healing or get taken out of that fiery furnace, do you display your gratitude publicly? Others need to hear your testimony. **Revelation 12:11** tells us clearly, ***"They triumphed over him (Satan) by the blood of the Lamb and by the word of their testimony."*** Wow! That's how important our testimony is; it is in the same sentence as the blood of the Lamb. Our testimony is full of power; enough to make the darkness of the world flee. Darkness cannot remain where the Light of Heaven shines. Don't be one who prays vehemently for a miracle only to refrain from telling others about it when it happens! Don't forget to give thanks vehemently. There are many who might be going through what God brought you through – they need to hear or read about it and then, like that one leper, your *faith will make you well.*

Going back to the story of the ten lepers, only one, who was a Samaritan came back when he saw he was healed. He came back, praising God in a loud voice. He threw himself at Jesus' feet to display his gratitude. *"Jesus asked, "Were not all ten cleansed? Where are the other nine? Has no one returned to give praise to God except this foreigner?" Then Jesus said to him, "Rise and go;*

your faith has made you well." **Luke 17:11-19**. This story shows us that Jesus appreciates the gratitude we display to bring glory to His Father after a miracle. Your faith has made your well is underlined. What if the Samaritan leper received more than the other nine by being made well? The other nine received a physical healing from leprosy but they did not receive the entire blessing of being made spiritually well because they did not come back to give thanks. To be made well by Jesus – ***Isn't that what we all want?***

Aging Gracefully

Display a spirit of gratitude especially as we age; You don't want your new nickname to be 'Grumpy Pants'. Be someone that people want to be around rather than getting your face stuck in a gear that sounds cranky. Keep in mind a bad attitude is like a flat tire, you can't go anywhere until you fix it. Rejoice! This is the day the Lord has made . . . and it might be your last one.

We are one day closer to the Kingdom. Smile through those dentures or those six remaining teeth. Be grateful when your see those wrinkles on your face – they are *wise* cracks. Admire your hair color so full of *wisdom* highlights. For us balding men here's a remark from my Tio Joe (Pipi): "my new hair color will soon be beige." (He was referring to his increasing loss of hair and display of more beige skin). Put on some pomade or Tres Flores on your head in case it turns into out to be a windy day. There might not be a lot of hair to hold down, but it makes the balding head shine and it smells like you still care about how you look.

Lastly, choose *wisely* and stay within your limitations. Don't attempt to do more than you once could. We got to this age by making *wise* choices. We are survivors! The passing mark of survivorhood (new word) will come when you hear the words, "Well done, my faithful Servant!"

Famous last words before a visit to the emergency room.

Grandson: "Tata, you're too old to ride my skateboard!"

Tata: "Hold my Ensure!" (I used to say, "Hold my beer!")

If you're blessed enough to reach seventy and no longer have to punch the timeclock, you have to make a choice each morning. You can spend the day in bed thinking about the body parts that ache and don't work like they used to, . . . Or you can jump out of bed and be thankful for the parts that still work. However, jump out of bed slowly and make sure both legs aren't in one pant leg before you take that first step in the morning. LOL

Every day is a gift as long as your eyes open, search for miracles and S.M.I.L.E. - See Miracles In Life Everyday. My vow is to focus on the new day by being grateful for second chances. My prayer is to share my gratitude through writing all to bring glory to God. Trust God, Believe in Jesus, Read your bible, and begin each day with a grateful heart.

Salvation Station Lesson # 10 . Faith cannot operate in an environment contaminated with bitterness and unforgiveness. It is activated by gratitude and obedience.

Recommended song to *tune you into the wisdom* about the message in this chapter is: **Worthy Is The Lamb by Hillsong United and Delirious.** It can be found on YouTube. Some versions include the lyrics.

CHAPTER 11

BORN ONCE, DIE TWICE (SECOND DEATH)

"The one who has an ear, let them hear what the Spirit says to the churches. The one who overcomes will not be hurt at all by the <u>second death</u>." **Revelation 2:11**

No one likes to talk about death but we all know it is inevitable. In fact, statistics show that one out of one person's die. My calling as a spiritual leader is to explain three types of death that a person can experience. Physical death, spiritual death, and Eternal or the second death. Along with this explanation I will elaborate on what I mean by Born once, Die Twice. This also means that if you are Born Twice, you Die Once. Please tune in as I have prayed to find the words to explain this properly and understandable. Below are the three types of death in the physical and spiritual realm.

1. *Physical death* is the separation of the body from the spirit. This human death is easy to comprehend as most of us have been to funerals or had a loved one die. As a young boy it really terrorized me to hear the wailing that took place at a viewing of the deceased. Most of the services I attend now are a celebration of life where memories and photos are shared. Believers burying believers know physical death is not final and it is more of a see you later instead of it being the last time you see them. My tio politico (uncle Mike

Gonzales through marriage) likes to tell me as we are saying our farewells: "I'll see you or you'll see me!" I asked him what he meant by this and he explained, "If I'm in the coffin, you'll see me but I won't see you or vice versa." He laughs because he knows we are both going to Heaven and we have no fear of death.

Currently life expectancy for a typical man in the United States is 78 years. Let me see, 1952 + 78 = 2030. Oh good, that gives me time to continue writing and sharing the Good News of Jesus. I will continue to speak Jesus until I cannot talk or write any more.

2. *Spiritual death*, the way all of us are born, is the spiritual separation of each of us from God. When we are physically born, we are spiritually dead because of the original sin that was passed down from Adam and Eve. This original sin is in us and comes with a tainted nature that can only be removed by regeneration (being born again/twice). Regeneration is explained in more detail in the next chapter. A person who does <u>not</u> believe God sent His Son to save us remains spiritually dead as the original sin remains. At some point, every person will make a choice that determines where they will spend eternity. Heaven is real and unfortunately for many, so is Hell.

3. *Eternal death*, or the second death, is the perpetual separation of a person from God. There is no escape from the second death. This death is the ultimate and permanent form of separation. If a person dies in a state of spiritual death, they enter eternity separated from God. Once a person has experienced the "second death" there is no hope for them, it is irreversible. It really saddens me to write this because I know many believe they can spend time in purgatory to pay for their earthly sins. Please take time to look for yourself if you believe in purgatory. I have read the entire Bible several times and did not find it mentioned.

Unless spiritual death is reversed in this earthly life by being ***born twice*** or born again, the result will be the second or eternal death. This results in a never ending separation between God and all who reject Him. So again, I write if you are born twice, you die once, however if you are born once, you die twice.

Physical Death is a Transition into Eternity

When we croak, push daisies, sell the farm, take a dirt nap, whatever you want to call it, we will spend eternity with God or be separated from God forever. When we are absent from the body, we are present with the Lord. The best Biblical example is when the crucified, penitent thief asked Jesus to remember him when He entered His Kingdom. Jesus reassured him that he would be with him by saying, "Today you will be with me in Paradise."

It is difficult to bury someone you love, however; our faith reassures us that we will meet again. The transition is easier when you know that the deceased was a believer. The joy of the Lord is our Strength when we celebrate the life and death of a born again believer. Jesus said, *"I am the resurrection and the life. The one who believes in me will live, even though they die, and whoever lives by believing in me will never die."* **John 11:25-26** When we believe in Jesus, we die once physically because we were born twice. Burying someone is even more difficult when laying to rest someone who has not been born again.

<u>Believers Are Not Affected by the Second Death</u>

"Blessed and holy are those who have part in the first resurrection. The second death has no power over them, but they will be priests of God and of Christ and will reign with Him for a thousand years." (**Revelation 20:6**).

As kids growing up in the barrio, we would do things to impress or irritate each other. One of the things we loved to do was to play with matches. It was an adventure to get outside undetected with a fresh, full matchbook and even better when you snagged some with the wooden match sticks. Somewhere along the way, one of my homies once asked me, "Have you ever seen a match burn twice?" I said no. He said, "You have to watch this very closely for this to work!" He then proceeded to light the match as I looked intently on the burning flame. He then blew out the match and quickly put the still hot match head on the top of my hand. He laughed and said, "Now you have seen a match burn twice!" This only happened to me once because it is one of those: -- 'fool me once -shame on you, fool me twice, shame on me travieso lessons'. This childhood lesson caused some minor pain on my skin but is nowhere near the agony caused by the lake of fire.

Lake Of Fire

The final judgment, or the lake of fire, is the time when the second death occurs. Read about it in complete detail in the book of Revelation in Chapter 20:11-15. It tells of the judgment of the dead and what happens to those who do not have their name written in the book of life. Anyone whose name was not found written in the book of life was thrown into the lake of fire, also known as the second death. Please make time to read this, *it is a matter of life and second death.*

In this chapter, you will also read how the devil is defeated and is thrown into the lake of burning sulfur. I know this sounds like the Twilight Zone but it's all there in Chapter 20 of Revelation.

"Then death and Hades were thrown into the lake of fire. The lake of fire is the *second death*." (Revelation 20:14).

The second death is reserved for unbelievers. Those who experience this death are all those whose names are not found written in the Book of Life. Those whose names are written in the Lamb's (Jesus) book of life are those who belong to God. *"Yet to all who did receive him, to those who believed in His Name, He gave the right to become children of God."* **John 1:12**

"But the cowardly, the unbelieving, the vile, the murderers, the sexually immoral, those who practice magic arts, the idolaters and all liars - their place will be in the fiery lake of burning sulfur. This is the second death." (Revelation 21:8).

The second death is even more painful because it is separation from God without hope forever. I recently heard a story of a well-known comedian who suffered serious burn wounds in a domestic fire. He had to receive skin grafts and treatment in a bariatric chamber to ameliorate the healing process.

This bariatric chamber was enclosed in glass as oxygen was released inside the hollow space. The comedian had to spend 8 hours per day and could see his caretakers but could not talk to them. He said this inability to communicate was worse than the pain from the burns on his body. He would try to tell them it was hot in the chamber but they did not understand. His isolation and no communication was minor compared to what eternity separated from God will be like.

God loves everyone and wants everyone to come to repentance. He is God and can bring on the rapture at any moment He chooses. ***"The Lord is not slow in keeping His promise, as some understand slowness. Instead He is patient with you, not wanting anyone to perish, but everyone to come to repentance."* 2 Peter 3:9**

Lost in an Urban Forest

One of the things I love to do in my retirement is to go walking. Sometimes my best ideas and creativity come during a long walk. It allows me to listen to music or the Bible app while enjoying the beauty of nature. I've done lots of walking in 2022 and will achieve my goal of 10,000 steps per day for the entire year. I set this goal because it was the year I would turn 70 if God allowed it. Last year, my average was a measly 7845 steps per day or two million eight hundred sixty three thousand four hundred and twenty five steps for the year. I've worn out a few pairs of Keds during the past two years. Maybe in 2023 I'll keep track of the number of salads I eat to better improve my overall fitness. This is just a passing thought because it is easier to track steps and tacos than it is to keep track of salad consumption. LOL

Perhaps I can finally apply what I learned at the University of Colorado to come up with a formula to find the breaking point on calories in the Taco to Salad ratio. It would look something like this: Taco squared divided by

Salad plus duration of exercise equals +/- weight gain. Somewhere in this equation the algorithm of leading someone to Jesus must be included. This overrides all other factors of this Taco to Salad spiritual equation.

Have you ever been lost as an adult? It can be really stressful and make you feel like you are losing your mind. Not too long ago I went for a walk in an area of Northwest Austin in a mini forest of cedar trees. Achoo! I could tell this area had been used by thousands before me. The trails were grooved like the ground underneath a 1960s merry-go-round in front of a drive-in. (**Yo! Youngsters!** This is how movies used to be watched instead of ordering them on demand) In one part of this cedar jungle, the path went into many directions. I was so far into the trees I could not see past the forest and there was no one around. The sky was cloudy so I could not rely on the sun for directions and the trees towered over me. I also forgot my walking stick that has a compass embedded into it. A sense of panic engulfed me as my phone had no signal and the only sound I heard was the ringing in my ears. I did the best thing, I sat on the ground and dialed into **SKY-FI**. This connected me to God and made me get rid of irrational thoughts like "Will I ever eat again?"

Before too long, I was having a good time as His presence was around me and nothing else really mattered. My praise to God began with a simple, 'Sing alleluia to the Lord'. Always remember, no matter how bad things look, even in your most desperate hour, lift your arms up in praise to our Creator. The promise in the Bible says nothing can separate us from the Love of God. My special time with God helped me get anchored. *Prayer is the anchor that keeps our soul from being shipwrecked when the storm comes.* Thank you, Lord, for hearing me when it looked like there was no way Home. I was probably lost for about 27 minutes but who's counting. LOL.

Pretty soon, a man came by and pointed me in the right direction to where I had parked near the entrance to this area. Faster than I could stand up (it's a long way up from the ground at age 70), he was already gone. I'm glad there was no need for Irma to have a silver alert issued for me that day. If I would have panicked and had started yelling 'HHEELLPP!' it would have ruined my reputation as a barrio boy extraordinaire.

There is another point I want to make in this story; there is only One Way to get to the Father even though some religions offer other paths. Jesus said it Himself: *"No one comes to the Father except through me*!!!" Some people think if they do more good than bad, they qualify for Heaven. Good deeds won't get you to Heaven; neither will regular Sunday church attendance, singing in the choir or following the Ten Commandments. You must *confess* with your mouth and *believe* in your heart that Jesus is Lord and God raised Him from the Dead. He is not one of the ways to Heaven, HE IS THE ONLY WAY!!! We are free to choose what path we want to follow in this life. However, we are not free from the consequences of our choice. Are you currently lost in an urban forest? How about in a country forest? There is a Way out, His name is Jesus.

Be Like Lee Roy

We call each other Primo (cousin) because his last name is Morales just like my middle name. I met him through his purchase of my books in 2020. We have gotten together for lunch on several occasions over the past three years. He lives in San Antonio and we meet halfway in between for lunch in San Marcos. Lee Roy takes care of his 88-year old mother and calls her his Queen. Earlier this year, he sent me this following email: Hey Primo …YOU'LL NEVER GUESS WHO'S NAME IS PRINTED IN THE BOOK OF LIFE AS OF TODAY AT 1:15 PM? The email was to tell me his mother accepted Jesus as Lord and Savior. Lee Roy had been worried as she had a couple of bouts with illness during the past year. A friend (Aurora) of his mom's cousin Celia just happened to visit his mom and presented the Good News of Christ in a simple, understandable manner.

Lee Roy enjoys hunting for a bargain and loves to collect antiques only to give them away. My tree in the back yard is adorned by a rustic bird house with a vacancy sign on it. If the birdhouse could talk, it would say: *"I'm so old, I knew the Dead Sea when it was sick!"* He was also kind enough to make Irma a custom-made dragonfly with ceiling fan blades used for the wings. He even painted it in her favorite colors of red and yellow.

On one of our lunch outings to San Marcos I asked him to tell me about when he became a born again believer. Lee Roy told me he was a truck parts salesman and he had lunch with a customer, a diesel mechanic named

Lou. (His actual name is Guadalupe Briseno.) After lunch, Lou asked Lee Roy questions about what would happen to him if he passed away while being in the religion he was currently in.

In Lee Roy's words, he responded, "I'm not a practicing Catholic, it's just what we were brought up in. We just followed the steps and went through the motions. Early baptism as a baby, first holy communion, confirmation, confession, etc." Lou then asked the pivotal question, "Where are going when you die, to heaven or hell?" Lee Roy was somewhat annoyed by this blunt question and answered, "Heaven of course because I am a good guy and not a bad person at all!"

Lou went on to tell him, "The Bible says the only way to heaven is through Jesus Christ. We have to accept Him as Lord and Savior!" Lou touched on other things about Christianity that Lee Roy could not remember in detail. *The bottom line was where would he spend eternity. Lou went on to say he had to make a decision soon because we never know when we will take our last breath.*

Lee Roy was standing there without giving an answer just thinking about all he had been told. Then **Lou did this: He made a line on the concrete floor of the mechanic shop. He then said, "On that side where you are standing is you and your life now. On this side where I am standing is salvation. You must make a choice NOW! Eternal life or eternal death?" Lou stood there with his arms crossed looking at Lee Roy and waiting for his decision.** *Lee Roy was not ready for this and could not decide. So, he told Lou, "Look I gotta go, need to make some more calls." Lee Roy jumped into his company truck and drove away. As he pulled away, he saw the reflection of Lou in his side mirror still standing there with his arms crossed.*

*After he had driven a few miles down the road his mind was full of conviction because he could still hear Lou's words ringing in his head. Lee Roy took a U-turn at the next light and headed straight back. As he pulled into the loading dock at the shop he was surprised to see Lou still standing there with his arms crossed. He now had a 'cat swallowed the canary' smirk and not a word was spoken. Lee Roy proceeded to the spot where Lou had drawn the line as Lou followed him and went to the opposite side of the line. Reflecting on the words Lou had said, '**eternal life' was there for the asking.*** *It all made sense to Lee Roy so he stepped over the line looking down to make sure he was across. When he looked up, he saw Lou with the* *biggest smile on his face. He reached out and hugged Lee Roy and said, "Welcome to the Kingdom of God, my brother." He proceeded to lead Lee Roy in reciting the prayer of salvation. Lee Roy immediately felt a heavy load being lifted from his shoulders. Lou invited him to church with his family the following Sunday.*

After they spoke for a while, Lee Roy drove off a second time. As he drove off to his next customer, the day was so beautiful and the sun seemed so much brighter. He felt like he was driving on cloud nine . . . everything was different, for the better. And in closing Lee Roy says, "And that's my born again story, and I'm sticking to it."

It was Lee Roy's day of Salvation as he asked Jesus to come into his heart. ***"But if Christ is in you, then even though your body is subject to death because of sin, the Spirit gives life because of righteousness. And if the Spirit of Him who raised Jesus from the dead is living in you, He who raised Christ from the dead will also give life to your mortal bodies because of His Spirit who lives in you."*** **Romans 8:10-11.**

In Romans 8:10-11, the apostle Paul teaches that Christ and the Holy Spirit work together in applying the resurrected life of Christ into the new believer. The Spirit's presence now is a guarantee of the future bodily resurrection of the believer. Lee Roy's name is written in the Book of Life as well as his 88-year old mother who accepted Christ on August 22, 2022. As believers, we become heirs of God's rewards in Heaven and patiently wait in hope for that glorious Day. Be like Lee Roy and his mom and receive the free gift of Life while you still have time on earth to make this decision.

Until the Very End

I was just getting comfortable to watch my favorite team on the last Thursday Night Football game of the season. The chicken wings were ready and so were the Dallas Cowboys. My cell phone rang as I had just opened a cold Topo Chico. My phone screen let me know the call was from a former co-worker. He had just accepted Christ about three months before after I presented him with the Good News in a church parking lot. He refers to me as "extension cord" because I have prayed for his son and aunt and they recovered from illnesses. I mentioned to him that I am just an extension cord to connect to Jesus, the power comes from Jesus and not from me.

He voice had a hint of desperation as he told me his stepfather was on his deathbed and he had a two-hour drive to make to a town near the Texas Panhandle. He had previously told me his stepfather was ill with ALS or better known as Lou Gehrig's disease. (This disease results in the progressive loss of motor neurons and continues until the ability to eat, speak, move, and finally the ability to breathe is lost.) My co-worker relayed to me that he was told his stepfather was alert but very weak. He went on to tell me his stepfather was a brilliant man but was anxious because he did not know what to expect after death so he was hanging on.

I told my co-worker, who is like my son, that as long as he is breathing, he can hear you. I told him about the night Jesus was saying goodbye to His apostles and referenced John 14. I emphasized how important it was for him to read John 14:1-6 out loud to his stepfather. (This is the same story I used to lead my father to Christ more than twenty years ago.) I reassured him to use his Bible and pray out loud so he could hear it clearly. My co-worker was extremely grateful and armed with the Word to speak to his stepfather as he continued on his trip to the Texas Panhandle. He told me he felt way better now that we had spoken and thanked me.

I followed up by sending him the following text message verbatim:

Read John 14 verses 1-6. After you read this ask him if he wants to follow Jesus into Heaven. If yes, pray with/for him. Tell him you are praying for him. Here's a simple prayer:

"Lord Jesus, I know that I am a sinner.

I know that you died on the cross and God raised you from the dead.

Please forgive my sins. I acknowledge you as Lord and Savior – I want to follow you into Heaven."

I told him to call me if he needed to as I would be up for a while.

Later after arriving at the hospital, my co-worker let me know his stepfather was alert but in a lot of pain. His stepfather kept blinking his eyes as he prayed aloud for him.

The hospital released his stepfather to go home the next day (Friday) in his right mind but not much left in his body. My co-worker let me know his stepfather passed away on the following Monday just before lunch. I sent him a message and said I was sorry.

The response I received was a text message: Don't be sorry, thank u, he was prayed for because of u. (*I know it was not because of me, but because of Jesus. All glory to the Lamb of God!!!*)

Praise God, the angels rejoiced as his stepfather was welcomed into Heaven.

Salvation Station – The Cross

One of the criminals who hung there hurled insults at him: "Aren't you the Messiah? Save yourself and us!" But the other criminal rebuked him. "Don't you fear God," he said, "since you are under the same sentence? We are punished justly, for we are getting what our deeds deserve. But this man has done nothing wrong." Then he said, "Jesus, remember me when you come into your kingdom." Luke 23:39-42

Jesus' life was draining out of Him as He was nailed to that old, rugged cross. I wish I could paint the look in Jesus eyes when He told the repentant thief. *"Jesus answered him, "Truly I tell you, today you will be with me in paradise." Luke 23:43* Jesus wants us all to live in Heaven with Him. That is why He sacrificed Himself for us.

Somewhere in Heaven today that same thief is admiring The Pearly Gates with the look of love for our Savior. Wonder if he still walks like he grew up in the hood? No matter if you have been bad all your life, all you have to do is ask Jesus for forgiveness and acknowledge Him as Savior. This convinces me more than ever there is a chance to our very last breath that we can ask for forgiveness and receive it. Nothing, no matter what we've done: *"Neither death nor life, ... will be able to separate from the love of God that is in Jesus our Lord."* **Romans 8:38-39**

The unnamed criminal probably did many bad things in his life to get crucified. He made his best decision when he believed in Jesus just moments before he died. That thief was *born twice* just before he succumbed on the cross, therefore, he only *dies once.*

Salvation Station Lesson # 11 If a person is dying and still breathing, there is still a chance for that person to be born again.

Recommended song to *tune you into the wisdom* about the message in this chapter is: **Forgiveness** by Toby Mac. You can find it on YouTube with lyrics.

CHAPTER 12

GLORY TO GLORY

"And the LORD God formed man of the dust of the ground and breathed into his nostrils the breath of life; and man became a living soul." **Genesis 2:7**

How can you give glory to the One who already owns all the Glory?

When God created the earth, it took six days and on the seventh day He rested. God made mankind on the sixth day. You can read the creation story in the first chapter of the book of Genesis. *"So God created mankind in His own image ..."* **Genesis 1:27a**. We are blessed to be created in His image. His Fingerprint image, *His Glory*, and perhaps His DNA, is inside all of us. We are blessed and He loves all of us the same. Believers will one day see Him in His full glory.

Every breath we take on earth is a blessing. Every day is another page in the book of our earthly life. Live each day so your last chapter has a great ending. That way when you wake up on the other side, you take the first step of your Golden Walk on the Street of Gold.

Only God can make a heart start beating. Only God can change a stone heart filled with anger and selfishness into one full of the Love of Jesus. Only God exhales His Breath of Life into a newborn baby as the infant takes its first breath. Only God inhales (takes back) His Breath of Life when we take our last breath.

Regeneration

Being born again in a new birth or *regeneration* is an act that only God can perform in which He renews the human heart. God acts at the origin and deepest point of the human person. This means there is no preparation nor a preceding temperament in a sinner that requests a new life given by God.

This new birth is necessary because all descendants of Adam and Eve have inherited their sin and this sin keeps us separated from God. *Regeneration* is the free gift of God's grace. It is immediate and supernatural through the work of the Holy Spirit. It awakens us from spiritual death to everlasting life. God has done His part by giving us His Son. It is our responsibility to become born again *by faith* in Jesus. The fruit of regeneration is faith. Regeneration comes before faith. And *without faith*, it is impossible to please God.

You probably have heard of how people are categorized into groups based on when they were born. A chart is shown below for a clearer explanation.

Generation name	Births start	Birth ends
The lost generation, or generation of 1914	1890	1915
The interbellum generation	1901	1913
The greatest generation	1910	1924
The silent generation	1925	1945
Baby boomers	1946	1964
Generation X (baby bust)	1965	1979
Xennials	1975	1985
Millennials / generation Y / generation next	1980	1994
iGeneration / Generation z	1995	2012
Generation alpha	2013	2025

What we need is an overlapping, all-inclusive generation called the free generation or Fre*Generation* (**pronounced free generation**). Free is good, freedom to be vocal about what we believe. Free to believe in the truth that will set us free. We are no longer chasing perfection because He loves us just the way we are. We have His love so we can go ahead and be who

He made us to be. It changes everything – there is no more guilt, no more shame; He took it all away!

It is based on regeneration or being born again in Christ. Part of this truth is knowing what we are living life for, that is: *"to love the Lord your God with all your heart and with all your soul and with all your mind. Love your neighbor as yourself"* **Matthew 22: 37–39**. Please understand, *we are not human beings having a spiritual experience but spiritual beings having a human experience.* Based on these convictions, choosing regeneration will determine where we will end up for eternity.

FreGeneration is the generation group I want to be associated with because it won't be too much longer before the Uppertaker (rapture) or undertaker (death) will take us from this earth. Join the army of the FreGeneration and accept the free gift of salvation. Then go tell others the Good News by being vocal about what we believe.

Living in Paradise

In the beginning at the Garden of Eden, Adam and Eve lived in complete peace with God. Their world was perfect. Adam and Eve were given one instruction from God, *"but you must not eat from the tree of the knowledge of good and evil, for when you eat from it you will certainly die."* **Genesis 2:17** So when they disobeyed God and ate from the tree of the knowledge of good and evil, they died spiritually and were banned from the Garden of Eden. This was the *beginning* of sin and as a result, we are born with this sinful nature. There was also another tree in the garden called the Tree of Life. If Adam and Eve had eaten from the tree of life, they would have lived forever. So, God placed cherubim at the east of the Garden to keep Adam and Eve away from the Tree of Life (**see Genesis 3: 22-24**) This was the *end* of their living in paradise.

But . . .*"God so loved the world that He gave us His only begotten Son, that whosoever believes in Him shall not perish, but have everlasting life."* **John 3:16** This is one of the most quoted scriptures in the Bible. The letters in John 3:16 are in red because Jesus was talking in His conversation with Nicodemus. Again, I remind you, Jesus told Nicodemus that a man cannot see the Kingdom of God except when a man is **born again**.

Do you believe in Jesus? Have you been born again? If yes, you will get to eat from the Tree of Life that is waiting for us in Heaven. This will be a great *beginning* to our eternal life. When we get to Heaven, we will get to see the throne of God and of the Lamb. Also, *"On each side of the river stood the Tree of Life, bearing twelve crops of fruit, yielding its fruit every month. And the leaves of the Tree are for the healing of the nations."* **Revelation 22:2** Those of us who have our names written in the Lamb's book of life will enter the New Jerusalem. This Heavenly City does not need the light from the sun or the moon because the glory of God gives it light, and the Lamb is its lamp. (From Revelation 21)

It's What You Do in Between the First and Last Breath

How do you give glory to the One who already owns all the Glory?

In our spiritual transformation as believers, we now have Father, Son and Holy Spirit making their home within us. Christ residing in our heart is as permanent, eternal, and spiritual as God Himself, rather than something temporary and earthly.

At some point in your life, you will make a choice for your eternity. *"Stand at the crossroads and look; … ask where the good way is, and walk in it, and you will find rest for your souls."* **Jeremiah 6:16**

The best decision I ever made was on November 13, 1999. My life completely changed as the old is gone . *"I have been crucified with Christ and I no longer live, but Christ lives in me. The life I now live in the body, I live by faith in the Son of God, who loved me and gave himself for me."* **Galatians 2:20** Always remember, *"Therefore, there is now no condemnation for those who are in Christ Jesus."* **Romans 8:1**

I still had so much to learn and was skeptical, but my heart was freshly plowed, and I was ready *"to live in safety and be at ease, without fear of harm." Proverbs 1:33* Little did I know that I had found Life and was about to learn about receiving favor from the Lord as paraphrased in the promise found in **Proverbs 8:35,** *"For those who find me find life and receive favor from the Lord."* *It was my beginning of going from Glory to Glory.*

At that time, I lived in Little Rock, Arkansas and Irma was 5 ½ hours away in Fort Worth, Texas.

Every weekend I made the roundtrip from Arkansas to Texas to attend church and Sunday School with Irma and Anthony. During one of my Sunday School lessons for New Believers, I was instructed it was imperative for me to read the Bible every day, so I bought my first Bible. After struggling with reading the Bible *every day*, and not even knowing where to begin, I sighed and gave a mental eye roll. I had my Gideon moment and I prayed something like this, *"Dear God, if you are real and your word is true, show me some proof."* I continued this prayer by saying, *"When I open my new Bible for the first time and touch whatever verse I land on, show me something that will increase my faith."* What happened next has led me to read my Bible EVERY day for the past 23 years.

When I opened my Bible, my finger landed on **Hebrews 4:12.** It says, ***"The word of God is alive and active. Sharper than any double-edged sword, it penetrates even to dividing soul and spirit, joints, and marrow, it judges the thoughts and attitudes of the heart."*** I was stunned and cried for nearly an hour as I knew this was not a coincidence but God caring enough for me to take me to this powerful verse. This was the first time in my life I felt oily tears flowing from my eyes. These tears seemed to cleanse my soul of all skepticism and disbelief. Hmm, here is a thought: ***If the eyes are a window to our soul, then perhaps our tears serve as the extra ingredient to see into heaven.***

Reading in the Good Book made me re-examine my beliefs. I was upset with some of what I had been taught in 1966 while attending a seminary in Compton, California. One of the first teachings at Dominguez Seminary was to pray the novena prayer on the back of a small card with a picture of the founding saint on the front. I was taught if I said this prayer for nine first Fridays and received communion, this guaranteed my admission to Heaven. I hope whoever reads this can understand how ludicrous and how off base this is. A set of prayers created by Anthony Claret will not get anyone into Heaven. He was the founder of the Claretian priests and nuns. He was born into a large Spanish family and lived from 1807 to 1870. He also founded a publishing company in Madrid, Spain that produced hundreds of Catholic books and pamphlets. He died at the monastery where he was staying in France on October 24, 1870 and is probably buried there. Like the apostle Peter said before the Sanhedrin, *"Salvation is found in no one else, for there is <u>no other name</u> under Heaven given to mankind by which we must be saved."* (**Acts 4:12**)

The reason I am writing about Anthony Claret is to point out the difference between this founder and Jesus. Anthony Claret, like every other religious founder, has died and stayed dead, but not Jesus. The resurrection of Jesus Christ makes Him different and superior to every person who has ever lived. All other religions of the world can point to a founder and then point to a grave or tomb. Only followers of Christ can point to an empty tomb and say, "Our founder is alive!" Jesus sits at the right hand of the Father in Heaven and scripture says in **John 12:32,** ***"And I, when I am lifted from this earth, will draw all people to myself."***

I read this scripture and the part: ***"when I am lifted from this earth"*** can be interpreted in different ways. It could mean when He was lifted on the cross during his crucifixion. The cross being a universal sign of Christianity. Perhaps it is about us lifting Him up in praise and worship to draw us closer to Him. It could also refer to His resurrection and conquering death. Maybe it is about His ascension into Heaven and preparing a place for us there. That is why I love to read the Bible because it is alive and active. The Word of God is ***sharper than* any double-edged sword; it judges the thoughts and attitudes of our hearts.**

My views on what I believe are Bible based and I have carefully examined what I truly believe. First of all, I believe Salvation is found in no other name but Jesus and *"**<u>Everyone</u>** who calls on the name of the Lord will be saved."* Romans 10:13. God loves us all the same and wants us to spend eternity with him. God examines the heart of every sinner, no matter what the sin is and grants forgiveness to anyone who sincerely asks for it.

Here is a list of what I believe (this paraphrases a song called **We Believe** by Newsboys.

1. **I believe in God the Father.**
2. **I believe in Jesus Christ.**
3. **I believe in the Holy Spirit and He has given us new life.**
4. **I believe in the crucifixion.**
5. **I believe Jesus conquered death.**
6. **I believe in the resurrection and He is coming back again.**

Here are some of the things I had to stop believing as I did not find them in the Bible.

7. **There is no purgatory.**
8. **Mary is not seated at the left hand of the Father. I honor her as Jesus' mother, but she was human. I did not find anywhere that she was given the position as sitting at the left hand of the Father. I was also unable to find any reference in the Bible about her assumption into Heaven.**
9. **You do not have to go to a priest to confess your sins.** *"There is one God and one Mediator between God and man, the man Christ Jesus." 1 Timothy 2:5*
10. **Praying to statues, saints, reciting novenas, rubbing beads or buddhas will not get you into Heaven. He said it Himself: "I am the Way, the Truth and the Life, no one comes to the Father except through me." John 14:6 also see Psalms 115:4-8**

This is not to say I am right, and you are wrong, but offering advice to examine your Bible and see what it says and what it does not say.

Early on in walking as a follower of Christ, my faith was enlarged by reading Proverbs and Psalms repeatedly over a three-year period. Did you know if you read five Psalms and 1 Proverb each day you will finish both books in a month? It seemed like every month I found new nuggets for my faith foundation. It was a process where the three steps to building my faith were: finding knowledge, receiving wisdom, and gaining understanding. It seemed like the more I read, I gained the understanding to give Jesus the full *glory*. My goal has now changed to doing what I can through my actions, prayers, and writings to point others to Jesus. Soli Deo Gloria – for the *glory* of God alone.

I've come to learn that I will never be perfect until I receive my glorified, heavenly body. I used to be full of guilt, regret, and feeling unworthy. One of my more recent Facebook postings summarizes where I am today:

<u>Walking in Wisdom</u>

No more darkness
Guilt has lost its grip on me
I still stumble every single day
I still get knocked down
But . . . the difference now is
That's not where I stay.
Cause I have a Savior
Who knows where I've been
And He reassures me
I'll never go back there again.
I'm walking in Wisdom, thank God!
~ *Ruben Gee*~

I've been fortunate enough to write about my Barrio Walk and I survived my Broken Walk. Today I remain on my Golden Walk and write about *tuning* others into Wisdom in Salvation Station. It's all for His Glory and to thank Him for the second chances he has given me. It's a continuous walk where I'm able to go from *Glory to Glory*. I like to look at things in the opposite direction. *Is it possible to go from unglory to unglory?*

Let's just say, you just came out of the seminary and you are no longer in the sheltered environment of no alcohol (unless you snuck a taste from wine used during Mass). You're curious and you want to fit in with your new friends at the inner city high school. You want to be part of the popular kids group. Here is the first step you take in going from unglory to unglory.

1. First beer
2. First drink of wine or whisky

3. Maybe some marijuana
4. How about some amphetamines to keep you awake
5. Cocaine, heroine
6. Expensive addictions with no money
7. Easy money by robbing, selling drugs, or stealing
8. Incarceration
9. Beat up and violated in prison (**NO**, I have not spent time in prison)
10. Hardness of heart
11. No way out – and separation from God

Please keep in mind, just because the past did not turn out like you wanted it to; it doesn't mean your future can't be better than anything you have ever imagined . . . Because you can go from unglory to glory. At any given moment you have the power to say this is not how my story is going to end. Make a decision to become a follower of Christ --- this is the first step on the *glory to glory* journey.

This is your responsibility and only works when you establish a personal relationship with the King of kings. It does not come because you repeated a prayer that was not sincere nor understood. Once you make that decision, you have to *stay connected* to Him for the remainder of your life. As you study more about Jesus' life, death, and resurrection, you will start building on the Chief Cornerstone. Each step forward begins your process of going from *glory to glory*. That final step, when you reach Heaven will be better than anything anyone could give you. "***What no eye has seen, what no ear has heard, and no human mind has conceived – the things God has prepared for those who love Him.***" **1 Corinthians 2:9**

Staying Connected

Don't you hate it when you need to get a message to someone and your telephone signal is going from one bar to no bars. You have probably experienced hearing a garbled telephone conversation at a time when you need to understand every word.

There have been times when I've called for technical support. The technical support person has used words like browsers and megabytes. In my 70-year-old mind, I have to trim my browsers regularly just like my mustache and megabyte is something I do at Wing Stop. Lol

Then there's those instances when you wait patiently on the phone to finally connect with that person from the IRS, DMV, or SSA, only to get transferred and disconnected.

So, what's going to happen if the power grid goes out and there's no internet, GPS, WI-FI, telephone, light, or Facebook? What if there's a trumpet sound and millions of people disappear including children that have not reached the age of accountability? What are you going to do if the rapture comes and you get ***Left Behind***?

What can you do then? What can you do now? Get connected to **SKY-FI** also known as prayer. Through prayer we have an instant 3-Way connection to God the Father, God the Son, and God the Holy Spirit. **SKY-FI** is available 24/7/365 and patiently waits for our connection.

You see, God loves us and wants us to spend eternity with Him. ***"God so loved the world that He gave His only begotten Son whosoever believes in Him will not perish and have everlasting life."*** **John 3:16**

And . . . NOTHING can separate us from the Love of God if we choose to use **SKY-FI**. There's no need for hardware, software, monthly payments, or technical support. *If you don't know how to pray just say Jesus.* Learn all you can about His Life, Death, and Resurrection.

No one goes to Heaven or Hell by accident, they go there because of a deliberate choice. That choice is to accept Jesus or deny Him. Jesus said clearly in John 14:6, "I am the Way, the Truth, and the Life. No one comes to the Father except through me." My prayer is to see you in Heaven.

God is the Alpha and the Omega . . . the beginning and the end. And . . . In the end – God wins and so do those who love Him and believe in His Son.

ADIOS

As I begin to say adios (goodbye) in this penultimate chapter of the book, please examine the Spanish word adios. If we say, "yo voy <u>a Dios</u>" it means I am going to God. "Vamos <u>a Dios</u>" means let's go to God. My prayer is we will all go <u>a Dios</u> at the end of our earthly life.

It is also God's desire that we live with Him for eternity . . . going from *glory to glory*. It was a glorious day when He sent His Son Jesus to live among us. It was a glorious day when Jesus completed His work on earth and ascended into Heaven. It is/will be a glorious day when we ask Jesus to come into our heart. It will be a glorious day when our earthly walk is over and we hear God say, "Bring out the best robe and put it on, my child." It will be a glorious day when we receive the Crown of Life for believing He sent His Son to die for us. It will be a glorious day when we meet up with other saints (family and friends) to eat from the sweetest fruit ever grown from the Tree of Life. There will be no taste bud remorse when we reach Heaven. On that glorious day everyone will be praising the Lamb of God, the One and Only – Jesus the Christ.

Tune into Wisdom as your life on earth and the life of others depend on it because it does and they do. As believers we must do everything we can to help others get connected to their personal Salvation Station. That Way we all go from *glory to glory* . . . all for the Glory of God alone. A-Dios!

Salvation Station Lesson #12 The gate to enter Heaven is narrow; stay on course by walking with a narrow gait. Keep walking using the Word to be a lamp unto our feet.

Recommended song to *tune you into the wisdom* about the message in this chapter is: **10,000 Reasons** by Matt Redman. You can find it with lyrics on YouTube.

CHAPTER 13

WHO'S KNOCKING AT THE DOOR?

"Behold I stand at the door and knock. If anyone hears my voice and opens the door, I will come to him and dine with him, and he in Me."
Revelation 3:20

Before beginning this final chapter of Salvation Station, I need to explain a term that came to me called *tastebud remorse*. It came after a meal I had enjoyed and had taken my last bite. Irma offered me what she could not finish and I blurted out, " No thanks, I don't want tastebud remorse." I hate it when I talk without thinking and then have to explain for fifteen minutes what I meant by my comment. Most people have experienced tastebud remorse but seldom talk about it and I've never read about it in a book. Tastebud remorse can come when you are eating pistachios or pecans and you put one of those hard to open or crooked ones to the side. You've eaten so many good ones, but the last one fills your mouth with that final, awful taste from a defective nut. Tastebud remorse can also come when you take that extra piece of food that should have been in a 'take home' box.

So, what does tastebud remorse have to do with Salvation Station??? In the opening scripture of this chapter, Jesus is knocking at the door of your heart. All you have to do is open the door and He will come in and *dine with you*. Please keep in mind, this is being written so you can examine your inner self in the spiritual realm. It makes me wonder if spiritually,

Jesus examines our kitchen prior to dining with us. What kind of fruit would He find in your heart? Would you hear Him say: *"I need to add more patience, faithfulness and self-control?"* (I'm referring to the nine fruit of the Spirit found in Galatians 5:22; the other six are *love, peace joy, kindness, gentleness,* and *goodness.*) Then after you dine together, does Jesus help us prepare better meals for us to share with others? Does He add more spices to our recipes? Does He somehow give us the desire to be more generous in sharing our food or putting it in our heart to pay for someone's meal?

As you invite Him in and He dines with you through the remainder of your life, you don't want Him to experience *tastebud remorse* after any meal. He is the Greatest guest you could ever have so always give Him your best. Let the Master Chef prune what He needs to take out of your kitchen (your life before Christ). That way you are worthy of partaking what He has prepared for you at your first Heavenly meal. It is only by opening the door to your heart to Him that you will be able to eat at His Table for eternity.

One of my newest best friends (Joel) and I have discussed how we make it a deliberate practice to leave the restaurant with that one last bite being what we liked best. Maybe it is dessert or eating that last bite of steak made perfectly to our liking. I know tastebud remorse sounds so *meaningless* like the word Solomon used repeatedly in the Book of Ecclesiastes. I want this final chapter to be a tasty morsel as you finish reading this book without having any *tastebud remorse.*

We Are In the Last Days

At this present hour, our world is flickering towards complete darkness from a spiritual perspective. We can see this in the circumstances that surround us in the natural. We must do all we can to nourish ourselves in the words of Jesus and seek the mind of God. We must be humble before God in reverent fear and ask Him for ample amounts of divine wisdom as we face the closing days of our lives. We only have a finite amount of time so we need God to "teach us how to number our days so we may gain a heart of wisdom." (Psalm 90:12)

When I meditated and prayed for a heart of wisdom to write Golden Walk, the prompting of the Holy Spirit told me to begin counting. As soon as I got to one, I heard the inaudible word, "STOP!" I stopped and pondered on the number one. The revelation felt like a stun gun zapped my brain. If I take care of one, (the only day I am guaranteed), everything else will fall into place. It's so simple, yet profound - count to *one* and take it one day at a time. Walk about in newfound freedom by walking in the spirit. Don't worry about tomorrow because today has enough to keep you occupied. God is in control. Take one step in the right direction by making one choice (Jesus). Follow Him one day at a time. He is the One Way for us to get to the Father. Enjoy the journey and help others get there. Let Him take your hand because He will not let go of you; if we take His Hand, we might let go of His when the storm is upon us.

Looking forward to that **One Day**

That One Day every knee will bow and every tongue will confess.
That One Day when our tired and weary bones find eternal rest.

That One Day when darkness and evil are put to an end.
That One Day when we'll see our promised land.

That One Day when there is no more pain, death, nor fears.
That One Day when His gentle touch removes all our tears.

Whatever God has for us in Heaven will make our eyes drool with delight.
And it lasts <u>forever</u>! Glory to God! Glory to the
Lamb! <u>Forever</u> in His Light! ~ Ruben Gee

Short-term Mission Trip

In September 2019, I was blessed with the opportunity to go with a team from Celebration Church on a mission trip to the Los Angeles Dream Center. **Caveat:** (Don't wait until you're 67 years old because the work is strenuous). What I saw through the eyes of my heart during that week left an imprint on my soul. I had the chance to do some introspection and learned I needed to make some adjustments to **fully serve God**. During that week, I cried inwardly and outwardly through the various emotions that brought new revelation. My eyes being the window to my soul, got a peek into Heaven as I added the extra ingredient of tears. Throughout my stay at the Dream Center, I experienced instances of praise, gratitude, compassion, joy, tiredness, brokenness, restoration, awareness, humility, abundance, peace and above all, His Love.

I learned the measure of love is Love without measure.

Receiving My Assignment

It was a morning filled with wonder as we prepared for going into skid row in the downtown area of Los Angeles. We wore Dream City shirts which are recognized by the homeless as "good guy" shirts. We had to be careful where we stepped because there were spots with puddles and no clouds in the sky. My eyes felt sympathy as we stopped and prayed for various individuals. I am thankful God gave me the boldness to pray without fear as it felt odd to have someone who is homeless clinging to me with their cheek pressed to mine. Somehow that morning my Spanish received a spiritual change of sparkplugs. I offered Hope to several who preferred to converse in the first language I learned.

We were giving away popcorn and water as we went by numerous tents. Many of the homeless wanted only water and tried to convince me to give them two waters and no popcorn. As much as I hated to, I had to ration the water so we could spread the blessing to as many as we could. My job was to pull the water wagon and I had to maneuver it on areas with dilapidated sidewalks. There was a faint smell of marijuana as we approached a park where we ended our walk in skid row. There was a basketball court and several areas for a large group of homeless people to sit.

Because I was pulling the water cart on the street, I was able to notice a man standing next to a port-a-john just outside of the park entrance on the edge of the sidewalk. He looked somewhat out of place as he wore a reflective vest like a person working for the City of Los Angeles maintenance department. I could not tell if he was one of the homeless, so I offered him my personal bag of popcorn that I had kept in case I needed to keep my energy level up.

He looked surprised and remarked, "No one from your group ever talks to me because they don't think I'm homeless. Even though dey come here every day, you are the first to offer me something!"

I told him, "Well that's probably because you have that nice vest on and look like a park maintenance worker." He promptly lifted his vest to display his overused shirt and pants that needed a couple of wash cycles.

He said, "I am homeless too!" with a faint Jamaican accent.

He told me his name was Ceven and I asked if it was spelled like the number seven. He became agitated and responded, "No! C-E-V-E-N" as he spelled it out loudly. He said he wished people would get it right. I quickly changed the subject, as I did not want to engage in a meaningless debate over the spelling of Ceven versus seven. He was aggressive and, in my BC (before Christ) days, we probably would have exchanged some unpleasantries that included badmouthing each other's mommas.

I asked him, "What do you do here?"

He said, "God gave me the assignment to keep this bathroom clean even though I don't get paid. I'm here every day and clean up mess after mess. It is not what I want do but God told me to do it so here I am."

I was stunned by this and told him about the Dream Center. He said he had never heard of it. I pointed out the two main leaders in the group that could offer him more information as I was only in Los Angeles for a week.

He seemed interested but told me "None of 'dem talk to me." He then went into a rant and repeated that even though he was homeless, they never talked to him.

I told him I was 100% sure, they would listen to him if he approached them. My prayer is this homeless servant of the homeless has gotten the help he needs.

Every night in bed, I reflected on what I experienced during that day. I would wake up almost nightly with cramps in my legs from walking an average of 16-18K steps per day. That particular night when I asked God why he connected me with Ceven, God was quick with His answer. He said it was to show me genuine humility. "AND, YOU NEED MORE OF IT." He reminded me of the second chance He gave me, and . . . forcefully told me I needed more humility. This hit me hard as God reprimanded me and gave me my assignment to fulfill for the remainder of my life. That is to write about Him and the second chance I received. My main purpose is to reach those, who were brought up like me, and never had the opportunity to hear the full salvation message.

I cried in my bunk bed that night when I realized I now knew what true humility was. My mind pondered, how can a person who is homeless devote his life to cleaning a public port-a -john on skid row? **The answer was humility and it crushed me to realize right then I needed more of it.** *Have you ever cried to the point where tears rolled into your ears?* I found out my purpose for the remainder of my life at the end of my tears. My last days on earth will be full of gratitude when I write and speak about His Goodness. My plan NOW is to talk about HIM every day until the undertaker puts me away or the 'Uppertaker' (rapture) takes me Home. My actions will display His Love through small acts of kindness, encouragement, and compassion.

After my time on this short-term mission trip, I immediately decided to retire so I could become a better witness through writing. My passion is to get Hope, Encouragement and Wisdom to a hurting world. I have been blessed with the social media platform on God's Wisdom United Facebook page. There are presently more than two thousand nine hundred individuals following the Wisdom United Facebook page. Wisdom United is built on the foundation in Colossians 3:12-14. As believers, we must clothe ourselves with compassion, kindness, humility, gentleness, and patience. We must forgive one another as the Lord has forgiven us. And ... over all these virtues put on Love which binds them all together in perfect unity. It is our vision to eventually sell product with all profit going to the truly needy.

That week at the Dream Center has fueled me over the past four years to write four books all for His Glory. The best part about writing these books is being able to donate any profit to charity. I am in awe that God has given me the privilege to write about Him, so I can tell of His incredible love for all of us. I gratefully accept the promise found in **Proverbs 4:11-13,** *"I instruct you in the way of wisdom and lead you along straight paths. When you walk, your steps will not be hampered; when you run, you will not stumble. Hold on to instruction, and do not let it go; guard it well, for it is your life."* I fully understand my ability to *walk about in freedom* only comes from receiving instruction from Him.

Seek Wisdom

When we seek wisdom, we are seeking the mind of God regarding earthly circumstances. If we walk in true wisdom, we are seeing things from God's perspective. There are benefits that come with finding wisdom. *"For through Wisdom your days will be many, and years will be added to your life."* **Proverbs 9:11**

You must first understand that Godly wisdom begins with reverence or to stand in awe of God.

"The fear of the LORD is the beginning of wisdom." Proverbs (9:10a) Unfortunately, we live in a world that does not value Godly wisdom even though it is more precious than rubies. Most people choose to go with the flow of society and rely upon "worldly" wisdom. That's what the flesh wants, but remember, your flesh will return to dust and will not make a transition into eternity. **When people live void of Godly wisdom, they embrace a life of folly. I know this personally because I was there.**

There are many reasons people choose to act and live foolishly, here are three I experienced:

- First, it came from not having the Word providing nourishment to my soul. Growing up I saw my dad and uncles always drinking on weekends, it seemed like the normal thing to do.

- I thought I was self-reliant. A young man thinks he knows everything and in the strength of his youth thinks he can do anything without God.
- I responded to peer pressure and societal pressure. Bad company corrupts good character. My mother used to tell me, "Show me your friends and I'll tell you who you are. We lived in the hood so there was always a plethora of hoodlums to keep company with.

STEPPING INTO WISDOM (SIX STEPS)

My first book called Barrio Walk: Stepping Into Wisdom describes what I experienced growing up 'south of the tracks' in Phoenix Arizona from age five to nineteen. (1957 to 1971). Looking back on my journey, here are six steps to steady your gait so you can walk through the Narrow Gate.

1. **You must commit to having a strong determination to walk wisely (Read Proverbs 2:1-7)** Walking in wisdom requires a decision and a commitment. You must settle it in your mind that God's way is the right way, regardless of how you feel about it.
2. **Pray for wisdom (Read James 1:5-8 and Hebrews 11:6)** The Bible is clear: *"You have not because you ask not"* (James 4:2) Come in faith before God in prayer and ask Him for wisdom. Our Heavenly Father is waiting for us to ask Him for wisdom.
3. **Meditate on God's Word (Read Psalms 119:97-105)** If you desire wisdom, you must devour God's Word. The more you come to know the Word of God, the more Godly wisdom will be available to you in times of trouble.
4. **Actively obey and apply God's Word (Read James 1:22-25)** True followers of Christ are called to put the words into action. Walk the talk then others will see your fruit which is a walking display of a life changed by God.
5. **Be sensitive to the prompting of the Holy Spirit** Walk by Faith and by the Spirit and obey the prompting of His voice even when it does not make sense, it will later. (**Read Ephesians 4: 26-29**) True wisdom recognizes the vital role of **the Holy Spirit** in daily life.

6. **Associate with, and learn from, wise people (Read Psalm 1:1; Proverbs 13:20)**

   Believers are warned throughout the scriptures to watch the company they keep. Share the Word and ask questions.

Below is a nugget of wisdom to guide you in life.

Always Remember, Knowledge is knowing that a tomato is a fruit.

<u>**Wisdom**</u> *is knowing that it does not belong in a fruit salad.*

<u>Knock, knock!</u>

Who's there? Guess what? It's not the big, bad wolf! This is not a fairy tale where the book ends and all live happily afterward. The knock is coming from Jesus asking to come into your heart – all you have to do is open the door and you will live happily ever after in a mansion He has prepared for His followers. This is the same Jesus sent from His Father, Our Creator. God gave us His Son. Will you receive this free gift of salvation?

Stop for a moment and wonder: How many people were there knocking on the Ark as water from rain was up to their ankles? There were probably numerous bloodstains caused by those knuckles of desperation on the side of the Ark as it began to float away from those that would perish. This is my **<u>bare bone plea</u>** for you to open your heart to Jesus. **We are in the Last days!**

The Lord will return when we least expect it. ***"Just as it was in the days of Noah, so it will be in the days of the Son of Man.*** *(when Jesus returns)* ***People were eating, drinking, marrying, and being given in marriage up to the day Noah entered the ark. Then the flood came and destroyed them all."*** Luke 17: 26-27

<u>Last warning – He Is A Jealous God</u>

In the second of ten commandments found in Exodus 20: 2-17, God spoke these words: *"You shall have no other gods before me. You shall not make for* *yourself an image in the form of anything in heaven above or on the earth beneath or in the waters below. You shall not bow down to them or worship them; for I, the Lord your God, am a __jealous God__, punishing the children for the sin of the parents to the third and fourth generation of those who hate Me, but showing love to a thousand generations of those who love Me and keep my commandments." * **Exodus 20:3-6**

What is the other god you might be worshipping before Him? What comes first for you before God? Is it your possessions, your job, your hobbies, your vices, your lifestyle, your pride, or your reputation? *Only you can answer that* and only you can prevent facing eternal fires.

I used to be in awe of some of the professional athletes on my favorite teams - They are just mortal men! One of my friends used to tease me and say I would trade my soul if the Suns could win a championship. Many years ago, when Charles Barkley was a member of the Suns, he said, "I am not a role model!" He was absolutely correct. Even though the Chuckster had superior physical skills, he did not always display the social skills to be worthy of being called a role model.

As a young man, my love for music of some of those worldly bands could have been considered idol worship. The songs, lyrics, and dancing in the clubs did not leave room for hearing the Word of God. So consequently, Faith did not come as a result.

We have to hear the Word of God and also share it if we care about the souls of those who may not have had the opportunity to hear the Good News. Consider this: *If your heart doesn't ache for people who don't know Christ, are you just hoarding Him for yourself?* The more we read, the more we can share.

Here is a final warning from Isaiah I found in the process of writing this book. I had read it other times, but this time around the words illuminated brightly. ***"The images that are carried about are burdensome, a burden for the weary. . . . Some pour out gold from their bags and weigh out silver on the scales; they hire a goldsmith to make it into a god, and they bow down and worship it. They lift it to their shoulders and carry it;***

they set it up in its place, and there it stands. From that spot it cannot move. Even though someone cries out to it; it cannot save them from their troubles." (Isaiah 46: 1b, 6-7)

Get rid of whatever you idolize. The greatest commandment from the new testament is to Love the Lord with all your heart, soul and mind and also love your neighbor as yourself.

Wake up sleeper! Don't continue to spend your life stuck in trying to gain the world while you lose what matters. If you're sleeping like I used to be, open your eyes. Open the door to our Savior knocking and promising to give you a brand new life. Then, you can thank God the Father for the Light of the World, His Son who got us out of the dark. Wake up to a brand new heart and a brand new life. Hallelujah! The old is gone and the new has come!

Who Saw Me When I Was There?

Picture this: I was once a 12-year old boy who would practice making mean faces in the mirror when no one was looking. I was worried about facing that bully again. *Who saw me when I was there? His name starts with a capital J but I did not know Him yet.*

Who saw me when I was in complete darkness and asleep in the car from one too many? Who protected me when they were trying forcefully to open my car doors? *Who saw me when I was there? His name starts with a capital J but I did not know Him yet.*

Who held my ship in the Hollow of His Hand while I served in Vietnam? Who helped me with my fear when we were in the state of General Quarters – battle ready and locked in a floating prison below the waterline of my watertight ship. *Who saw me when I was there? His name starts with a capital J but I did not know Him yet.*

Who heard my cry when no one else did in the middle of a full church at St. Patrick's Cathedral? *Who saw me when I was there? His name starts with a capital J but I did not know Him yet.*

Who came into my heart on November 13, 1999? He was always there and I know Him NOW. He is Jesus, my Lord and Savior.

If He did it for me, He can do it for you – all you have to do is answer His Knock and open the door to your heart. My life is living proof that Jesus can take anyone from lost to found. It doesn't end there; you have to stand firm until you reach Heaven.

In these last days, *"Put on the full armor of God, so that you can take your stand against the devil's schemes. For our struggle is not against flesh and blood, but against the rulers, against the authorities, against the powers of this dark world and against the spiritual forces of evil in the heavenly realms. Therefore, put on the full armor of God, so that when the day of evil comes, you may be able to stand your ground, and after you have done everything, to stand."* **Ephesians 6: 11-13**

I'm about to close this laptop and finish this book. When you read it, I might already be in Heaven because of my death or the Rapture came and many have disappeared. The world will be in chaos; but remember, God still loves you. During your last days on earth, as long as you are breathing, you can still make a decision to accept Christ as your Lord and Savior.

God bless you and your family. Until we meet at the Tree of Life, tell someone about how Jesus touched you.

Salvation Station lesson # 13 Jesus is waiting for you to open the door of your heart. All you have to do is open the door.

Recommended songs *to tune you into wisdom* and reinforce the message in this chapter are: **Walking Free** by Micah Tyler and **Wake up Sleeper** by Austin French. You can find these songs with lyrics on You Tube.

HOW TO FOLLOW
RUBEN GONZALES

You can order signed copies of his books or
read his blogs on his website at:
www.WisdomUnitedLLC.com

His email address is: Rubengee820@gmail.com send him an
email if you have any questions pertaining to his writings.

You can find his personal Facebook under Ruben M. Gonzales

He also has Facebook pages for Barrio Walk and Wisdom United.

**As information, all profit from book sales is
donated to charity. God bless you
and your family!**

Looking forward to **That One Day**

*That One Day every knee will bow and every tongue will confess.
That One Day when our tired and weary bones find eternal rest.*

*That One Day when darkness and evil are put to an end.
That One Day when we'll see our promised land.*

*That One Day when there is no more pain, death, nor fears.
That One Day when His gentle touch removes all our tears.*

*That One Day that I'll have even more than everything I have prayed for.
That One Day is just a mist away and has way
more than my mind can conceive.*

*Whatever God has for us in Heaven will make our eyes drool with delight.
And it lasts forever! Glory to God! Glory to the
Lamb! Forever in His Light! ~ Ruben Gee*

EPILOGUE

God is Faithful

A common question I am asked is: "How did you become an author?"

It was never my life intention to write books but it was more my desire to document memories about growing up in Phoenix, Arizona in the 1957-1971 timespan. I had no clue that I would write Christian books, as this is now my fourth because **God is Faithful**.

In my first book Barrio Walk: Stepping into Wisdom published in 2019, there is a story from 1971 where God arranged a meeting that unbeknownst to me would have a profound influence. On page 126, there is a short story of a visit from JD Hill to the inner city grocery store where I worked. The story finishes with this excerpt: *"That was one of my best days at Carlito's Market. Everyone in the store was impressed that the one and only JD Hill would stop by to see me and give me a jersey. At this point I had some serious "barrio cred."* Looking back on this meeting, it has orchestrated what my ministry would become in my golden years. Meeting JD Hill was a divine appointment because **God is Faithful.**

God's timing is much more different than ours so I fast forward to September 2019 or 48 years later. My manuscript for Barrio Walk was now complete and I tried to find JD Hill to obtain his permission to include him in the book. I was not able to connect with him at his ministry at the Phoenix Dream City Church, but don't worry because **God is Faithful.**

In October 2019, I was blessed to be part of a short mission team that went to the Los Angeles Dream Center. I had the privilege of meeting Global Pastor Tommy Barnett. During our conversation, I inquired about JD Hill and Pastor Barnett asked me how I knew JD Hill. I told him about when JD visited me and I was trying to locate him to obtain permission to include him in the book. Long story, short, Pastor asked me to send him a copy of the non-published manuscript for Barrio Walk. In a week or so, I received an email from Pastor Tommy's secretary that he wanted to endorse my book. What an awesome blessing because **God is Faithful.**

It gets better, Pastor Tommy Barnett endorsed Broken Walk: Searching for Wisdom (2020) and was kind enough to write the forewords for Golden Walk: Following Wisdom into Heaven (2021) and also for this book in your hands because **God is Faithful**.

The Phoenix Dream City Church blessed me with the opportunity to sell three books at the recent men's conference held on February 28 – March 1, 2023. And guess who the nearby vendor was?? The one and only JD Hill. It was the first time I had seen JD since 1971 or fifty-two years later. JD was selling his book called *Go Long – The Story of JD Hill*. It is an excellent book that needs to be shared with everyone to tell them there is always room for restoration, redemption, and renewal.

It was a special moment at the conference for me to spend time with and hear JD Hill read out loud from Barrio Walk about his meeting with me to his NFL friends. He was overjoyed and when he finished, he told me, "You have my approval!" Such a blessing from a seed planted in 1971 that fully bloomed 52 years later because **God is Faithful**.

God is Faithful!

04089960-00835930

Printed in the United States
by Baker & Taylor Publisher Services